To Win

THE CHRISTIAN'S PERILS, PRIVILEGES, PERFECTION, PEACE, POWER AND THE FULNESS OF THE SPIRIT

REV. W. P. NICHOLSON

Ambassador

FIRST PUBLISHED 1926 AS "ON TOWARDS THE GOAL"

AMBASSADOR PRODUCTIONS LTD.
PROVIDENCE HOUSE,
16 HILLVIEW AVENUE,
BELFAST BT5 6JR

Preface

The following pages reproduce a series of addresses delivered at the Bangor Convention of Easter, 1925. Mr. Nicholson is a man by himself, and has his own inimitable way of putting things, often racy, always forcible.

Before the Lord called him, his calling was that of a jolly mariner. His native humour and his facility in trenchant speech he regards as gifts to be consecrated to high ends. Some may question his judgement in this. But one thing is indisputable - that God used him mightily, in the spiritual transformation of Ulster.

"One thing I do . . . I press toward the mark for the prize of the high calling of God in Christ Jesus."

PHILIPPIANS 3 : 14

Foreword

I believe there was never a day or time when sermons such as these were more needed. We are truly living in "Perilous times." These are the "Last of the Last days," the "Love of many waxing cold," sinners deceived and deluded by a gospel which is not "The Gospel" into a false security. They are on the road to hell and do not realize it or believe it. Many are fully persuaded they are sure of heaven because they have been baptized and joined church and partaken of the Sacrament, while all the time they are merely baptized candidates for hell, eating and drinking damnation to their souls every time they sit around the Lord's table. I believe messages like the following are needed to sound a note of warning alarm. Their language is clear, plain and not easily misunderstood. Thet have had a world-wide ministry during the past 50 years, and greatly blessed of God to the salvation of thousands. There are messages here for spirit-born, blood -washed believers, declaring the urgent necessity for a sanctified, spirit baptized exprience, if we are to live holy, happy, useful soulsaving lives, worthy of the Lord unto all pleasing. There is no substitute for this blessing. It is the birthright privilege of every believer. Just as truly as regeneration is a necessity to a justified saved life, so sanctification is just as necessary for a victorious, holy life. These messages will surely urge and help believers along this truth. May the Lord richly bless these messages as they are launched out into this wider ministry and make them very fruitful in many lives.

Yours restfully busy,

WM. P. NICHOLSON.

JOHN 3 : 30

1
The Christian's Perils

I am going to speak to you, in these pages, about the Christian Life.

" But, man, you've spoken to us already about it, in yon wee blue book with the face on the front of it," you say.

Yes, I have, spoken about the Emptying and the Filling, the Overcoming and the Overflowing. But it is a subject of which I never tire, and I am continually seeing new aspects of it; so that what I have to say now will be quite different from what I have given before. I am going to shell some peas for you. The first P is the PERILS of the Christian Life, then we'll come to its PRIVILEGES, its PERFECTION, its PEACE, and its POWER. How will that do?

Well, then, let us look first at the Perils:

When you got converted, received Jesus Christ, the devil did not die. Sin has not been put into hell, where it will be put one of these days. You are in an alien country here, with an alien nature and an alien body; and you have, as such, inherited what will keep you busy for the rest of your days. Some people think they will never be tempted while they are Christians. You will not be long till you get an eye-opener. There are perils without and perils within, perils around, perils above and perils beneath. The reason why a good many people fail is their ignorance of these things; or, if not ignorant altogether, they fail because they underestimate their peril and under-rate the subtlety of the enemy.

If you are a nominal sort of Christian, a sham and a make-believe, whether a Methodist, Presbyterian or Church of Ireland Christian, you have a name to live while you are as dead as King Henry VIII. The devil will not bother you if you are unconverted. In shooting ducks, it is the wounded ones you run after: the dead ones can be gathered all in good time. If you are dead in sin, there are no perils, except the peril you will meet at the end. But for genuinely born-again Christians there are real perils. Let us look at some of them.

(1) There is first of all the peril of *unheeded self-discovery,* in which we fail to follow God's revelation about something in us.

Seven times the Lord tried to reveal to Judas what he was. You could not tell the difference between him and the rest of the disciples until it came to the end. Not one of them knew the difference. When the Lord said "One of you shall betray Me," consternation filled each of them. "Lord, is it I?" they all said. Seven times you have the Lord distinctly seeking to reveal to Judas the awful possibility of peril in his life; yet he shut his eyes to it, and rushed on to his doom and damnation. If the Lord has given *you* a revelation of anything wrong in yourself—in your nature, in your temper, in your tendency, in any way or manner, shape or form—it is a terrible peril to shut your eyes to it. Whatever weakness He may have revealed to you, whatever tendency, it is because the Lord sees it that He seeks to reveal it to you. It is a tremendous peril to refuse to see it.

You remember how, in the Old Testament, in 2 Chronicles, xxvi., a young fellow became king; and then, when he became lifted up, he sought to take the very position of the High Priest, although the Lord tried to show him the peril and to safeguard him against it. The danger lies with us to-day just as much as with those in olden time. The Lord sought to discover Peter to himself. "You are going to deny Me." "Deny You? I will *die* for You!" "Satan has desired to have you, that he may sift you." But, in spite of it all, poor Peter rushed on to ruin and sorrow. If the Lord shows us ourselves, it is a terrible thing not to pay heed to it. When you are at a railway junction, and the lines separate one from another, you know that at the beginning of their separation it is as sharp as the blade of a knife, but what a difference at the end! Beginnings may be very little in the matter of sin, but look at what they are at the end. If you are getting away from the main lines of truth, if you are getting wrong on any moral question, as you value your own soul, I beseech you to heed the Word.

When God gave Isaiah a revelation he cried "O Lord, I am undone! I am a man of unclean lips!" But he was in God's presence, where uncleanliness and undoneness could be cured. Just so with Paul. He cried, "Oh, wretched man that I am! who shall deliver me?" and then was able to say—"I thank God through Jesus Christ our Lord."

(2) The next peril is *presumptuous sin.*

There is more backsliding from this than from any other cause, especially amongst ministers and other workers. They argue, " The Lord used me in the past, and He is bound to use me again." " The Lord blessed me in my Sunday School class last Sunday and He is bound to bless me again." " I was all right with God yesterday and therefore I am all right with Him to-day." " Lord, save me from presumptuous sins! " cries the Psalmist. A lot of the hymns back this idea up, such as the one saying

" Each victory will help you some other to win."

That is a sentiment greatly open to abuse. I have only victory at this moment by this moment's faith in Christ. I have no victory to-day because I had victory yesterday. I have no triumph because I had triumph last week. There is nobody loves you like God, and He will keep you hanging in abject dependence on Him. " This is the victory that overcometh the world, even our faith." The weakest man or woman who has faith is as strong as all the forces of hell combined. It is not a question of your will or determination, or the strength of your jaw. It is not a question of the will to win—at least, not when it comes to salvation. When you and I get to the place where we rely on God completely, that is where our victory lies. But presumptuous pride says, " Well, I had a good time yesterday, and so I do not need to bother God by asking for grace to-day: I can get on fine." Ah, you will get a queer coup! You have to-day, and daily, to hang on to God; it is a moment-by-moment hanging on to Him. There is never a time when you and I can say we can lean on our past experience, or depend on our wisdom, or trust the arm of flesh. " Trust in the Lord with all thine heart and lean not unto thine own understanding."

A friend of mine in Chicago told me that learning this lesson cost him 250,000 dollars in one year. He owns cold storage plant, and he makes money fly for the Lord's work. Ultimately he became President of the Apple Growers' Association of America; and then he felt he was a very important man, and was inclined to say " This is me." He had to buy apples, of course, before they were grown; and he said to me, " Formerly I used to get on my knees and cry to God—' Should I buy that orchard, Lord? Should I buy that crop?' " But when he became president of the Apple Growers' Association he felt he did not need to ask the Lord, and that what he did not know about buying was not worth knowing. The result was that he dropped 250,000 dollars in one year. As a consequence he went back to his knees and God, and resigned the Apple Growers' Association.

It is sometimes unsafe for the Lord to bless a man. You remember that, in the case of Gideon, the Lord said, " I want to boil down your crowd,"—the crowd that had the fluttering around the heart. After that the Lord said " You have too many yet," and Gideon had to reduce the 10,000. And the Midianites were like the sand by the seashore! The Lord said: " If I gave victory by the 10,000, they would vaunt themselves and say ' We have got the victory.' " People sometimes say: " At the last Convention I got deliverance from my temper. I do not need to bother about it now, I got such a cleansing "; or, " I will never be bothered with doubts and fears, and never have any scare about whether anybody hears me sing, speak, or pray." You are in a perilous condition. Yes, one of the perils of your life, and mine, is that of presumptuous pride.

The mother and supposed father of Jesus went on their journey home " supposing Him to be in the company "; but they were wrong. There are many who often make the same mistake, even Keswick people. I have been twenty-five years on the job, and I am more helpless in God's hands than ever; but this spirit I speak of is the curse of the Church. " Oh, we know the kind of men that should be elders and deacons." But all we can see is the outside of the rascals. We are for showing God how to do things, and we make shipwreck of the whole thing. I don't know anything that the devil harps on more than that one thing—" Look at the success God has given you, look at your experience; you can take advantages and liberties with God." But in the sight of God we are all bankrupt. All our victory is of God, that no flesh should glory in His presence. " I have so managed to bring myself into control, my passions and desires, that I am quite safe," a man says; " I have got such victory over drink that I'm not afraid of it now." But by and by we find him drinking more than ever he did. We know what our lust and passions were, and if God does not hold us we shall be down. Some of the finest and biggest men in the highest positions have had the greatest falls.

I remember a fellow in California who professed sanctification. He said to me—" You are only half saved." But one day an accident happened to a load of peaches belonging to him, and when I arrived at that juncture I heard things coming out of his mouth that surprised me. He had spoken of the old man being dead, but I said to him—" What old man is that, that is going his mile now?" Our safety lies only in our constant abiding in Christ. There is no security in our wisdom or in our past experience.

(3) The peril of *uncounted cost.* It is one thing to make a start. The first step is not the hardest, but the last. "Lord, I will follow Thee whithersoever Thou goest," protested one candidate; and you know the reply: "The foxes have holes and the birds have nests, but the Son of Man has not where to lay His head"; and then it was "Good-bye, Jesus."

When the storm occurred on the lake there may have been an inclination to say, "Thank you, I am a fair-weather Christian." But "Except a man forsake all that he hath, he cannot be My disciple; except a man deny himself, and take up the cross daily, he cannot be My disciple. . . . Which of you, going to build, does not count the cost?" The Christian life is a life of battle and building and the Lord would have us to count the cost. Many a pilgrim has made a good start and a bad ending, because he did not count the cost of the persecution,—of being ostracised, maligned, misrepresented and hated of all men. It is better never to make the move than to make it and make a mess of it.

(4) *Unjudged sin.* Some of us preachers are awfully sore on other people's sins; but what about our own? Do you judge your sin? or do you treat it like a gouty toe? King Saul was delicate in handling the finest of the sheep, and spared them and Agag; but Samuel said—"In the name of God I will hew down Agag." Whatever sin God puts His hand on, are you as cruel as hell with it? or are you kind and do you pander to it?

The curse amongst us is a superficial sense of sin. We are playing with it, we have entered into a great sympathy with it, and we have all kinds of excuses and apologies to make for the accursed thing. God never condones sin; He forgives *sinners,* but He condemns and destroys sin. He hates sin with a burning white-heat hatred, and when you and I are as near God as we can get, we shall be inflamed not only with love, but with a hatred to sin. Do you make any allowance for it? How do you judge of it? Condemn it, in the name of God, and be done with it! It is a terrible peril, whether it comes in the shape of whisky, women, tobacco, worldliness, or anything else. If there is any sin in your life unjudged, drag it out and destroy it in the name of God. You may get a wound like a pin-prick, and before you know where you are you have got lock-jaw. President Coolidge's son had a blister on his heel, and in a fortnight he was a corpse. Sin is like that in its deadliness; it is a hellish thing: it will blight and curse, but never bless you.

People say—" Oh yes, I lost my temper, but I could not very well help it. Shake hands with me in my weakness."

Brother, judge the thing, unveil it in God's presence. There is a story told of an old Eastern monarch who was supposed to be beautiful—so much so that he kept a veil over his face lest beholders should be dazzled. But one day the veil was blown aside, and he was seen to be in reality what he was, an ugly rascal. Sin is like that.

(5) A *compromising policy.* Ask yourself,—Where will it end? Said a minister one day to me, " I want

you to do this and that"; and I said, "Well, sir, will you tell me where it will end?" I was not to preach so much about hell and damnation. I said, "You cannot deny that I preach the Gospel," and that was admitted. I said, "If I make this promise to you, where am I to stop?" That is the question everyone has to face.

You get an invitation to a card party, and of course you do not feel as if you were more holy than they. You have no love for the thing, but it is a delicate situation, and you say, "Well, I will go. I will not dance, I will just sit and look on; I will not play cards, but I will sit there. I want to show friendliness and I will go. I would like to help these friends of mine to Christ."

But you can never get a man out of a bog-hole by going in beside him. A lot of the so-called social work in churches is carried on with the motive, "We have got to keep the young people," and so we have all sorts of questionable things going on.

One minister put it, "After all, it is the same Gospel but it is a re-adaptation."

I asked, "How many are you getting with it?"

"Oh, well, not many yet."

"How many do you get out of that gang for the Prayer Meeting?"

"We have not got a Prayer Meeting."

The story of Abraham and Lot is not out of date. Lot said to Abraham:

"You will never do any good up here; the common-sense thing is to go down and make yourself one of them."

"No," said Abraham, "I will stay by my sheep."

Lot goes down, becomes a fine man in the cities of the

plain; but when the day of catastrophe draws near, Abraham has to pray for Lot: "Lord, be easy on them! Lot went down to do some social service work. If there are forty righteous people there will you burn them up?"

You know the whole story, and of how the children of Lot's daughters became the Moabites and Ammonites and were thorns in the sides of Israel ever afterwards.

People say to me, "Now, Mr Nicholson, would not you appeal to the better-class people if you were a little more considerate, if you would say 'condemned' instead of 'damned'?" A lady heard a canon preaching after she heard me, and she declared, "I would rather have the canon's hell than your's."

Oh, let there be a complete and constant abandonment to the Lord. It is not merely an act, but an attitude; not only a crisis, but a process; we should not only be filled with the Holy Ghost, but be in process of being filled. The crisis is when you make the surrender, and by faith receive; and the process is walking in the light as He is in the light and being filled with all the fullness of God day in and day out.

Take advantage of all the means of grace. If you begin to neglect private devotion, these perils will manifest themselves. Read your Bible. If you get into the habit of neglecting the means of grace and the Church, then look out! When a "twicer" at church becomes a "oncer," it is like Lot pitching his tent towards Sodom. People compromise by their Sunday reading, and by the use of tobacco for their infirmities. Get busy winning men and women to Christ, and try to get believers filled with the Holy Spirit. Remember, God has only one business, and that is saving men. For that one thing He gave all He had, and is doing all He can. God's work is a saving work. If you are not engaged in saving work, then do not say you are doing God's work. The only way you can keep a bicycle standing is by keeping it going; and we human beings are like that.

2

The Christian's Privileges

Ah, sure, it is a rich topic that I have for you in this Chapter—the Privileges of the Christian Life.

Let us start with some verses from the Apostle John, first epistle, third chapter—"*Therefore the world knoweth us not, because it knew Him not.*" What is the good of your trying to get the world to know you? Christ lived a sinless life among nine of a family, and they—at one time even His mother—" believed not in Him." The world knew Him not. Now, look down the chapter:—"*Whosoever keeps on sinning hath not known Him. Whosoever keeps on abiding does not keep on sinning. Whosoever keeps on sinning hath not seen Him or known Him. He who keeps on sinning is of the devil. Whosoever is born of God doth not commit sin,*"—that is, he won't live in sin. If I were to take a fish out of the water and put lungs in it, it would never live in the water again. Christ has taken me out of the old, and put me in the new, so that I could not live in the old now. Show me a happy back-slider, and I will show you a truthful liar, a virtuous harlot, and an honest thief. There are two families in the country, and two homes being prepared for them. There are also two fathers in the world. Cain was the first unbloody Unitarian. " Marvel not if the world hate you," you can go to your card parties, picture shows, and dances, and you will be a nice fellow; but if you are of God the world will hate you. Ninety-nine per cent. of the victory is a good knowledge of the kind of perils you are going to meet.

But I want to speak of the privileges, for there are many of them—the privileges or rights we may enjoy.

There are many living poor half-starved shadowed lives, down at the heel, beggarly, miserable, disgruntled and dissatisfied, because they are ignorant of their riches and rights. They are saying, " Give me a crust," when they might have " the unsearchable riches of Christ." Suppose I were a beggar and someone said to me, " Do they call you William P. Nicholson? "

" Yes."

" Do you not know your father died and left you twenty million pounds? "

If that were true I would be sailing down the road in a Rolls-Royce and have a new suit every day, and beef-steak and onions every day! You are a millionaire since the Lord has died. It does not matter how commonplace we are, we are wealthy beyond the wildest flight of imagination. And yet many are living like paupers, half-starved, half-blessed, to whom the Lord is merely of no form nor comeliness. Ah, if you only get to know something of your privileges and rights in Christ, you will see He is the chiefest among ten thousand and the altogether lovely, and you will begin to get something of what He has purchased with His blood, to show to the world what a wonderful Saviour He is.

What are those privileges? Here are a select few:

(1) A *filial relationship* with God. We were not naturally that way. You were born a child of the devil, a child of wrath, " by nature children of wrath even as others." There is a lot of rubbish talked as if every one was a child of God. God is not the *Father* of dogs and cats; He is the *Creator* of them. He is not the *Father* of the devil or the damned, but He is the *Creator* of them. There is not a child of God in hell, or on the road to it, and there never will be.

A dear old maid said to me once, " I suppose you have children? "

" Yes."

" I suppose you love them? "

" Yes."

" If your child was in pain, and you could alleviate it, you would do it? "

" Yes."

" You say God is a Father? "

" Yes."

" And God's children are in hell? "

" I did not say so."

She asked, " Who is in hell? " and I replied, " Children of the devil." The Lord has a home for His crowd, and the devil has one for his crowd. If universal fatherhood is right, then Unitarianism is right, and that is the main plank of Mohammedanism and the other isms.

When you repent of your sins and believe in Christ, when you come to the conscious realisation that you are a guilty soul and see in Christ all that your heart needs, you become a child of God. " As many as received Him, to them gave He the right to become children of God."

I met a woman in Glasgow once, who told me she had ceased to believe in the Lord and to pray. I asked her, "Why?" She told me her boy—her only son—had been drafted into the army and sent to France; and she had asked the Lord to spare him, and believed He would. But her boy was killed, so she threw up her "religion," and ceased to believe in God, or pray, or go to church, or read her Bible. "God doesn't answer prayer. It is no use praying or believing." She had thrown everything overboard.

I said to her: "Keep quiet a wee minute until I ask you a question: 'Are you born again?'"

She said, "I'm a Presbyterian."

"Never bother about that," I said. "Are you saved? Are you born again?"

"No," she said.

"Well," said I, "you were tugging at the wrong skirt, knocking at the wrong door, if God isn't your Father. Why didn't you apply to Satan?"

"I never heard the like of that!" she said.

Then I showed her her need, and how to be born again, and she entered into light; and now she has the privilege of a child of God, to present her petitions before Him.

Are you in God's family? You do not get there by your mother. When you were born by your mother you were born in sin. No wonder they put a black cover on the Bible, which reveals such facts. It is *by faith* that we are sons and daughters of the Most High. What a privilege! These worlds in space are all my Father's. Consider how rich I am because I am His son. When Adam got children it was in his own image; and when you are born again you are begotten into the very likeness of your Father; love and holiness are the outstanding characteristics of every born-again man and woman. It is not a question like adoption, like you taking a child that you know nothing about. No, I have the very nature and life of God; the same life that is in Christ is in me, and the same Spirit. It is a living, loving, and eternal union, the life that is put into you when you are born of the Holy Spirit.

(2) There is another privilege and that is our *access to God.* I do not need any old Pope, any man, or sacrament, or ceremony, to introduce me to God. The angels have to veil their faces; but when I go in it is " with unveiled face." The high priest only went into the Holy of Holies once a year; but I *live* there. Glory to God! " He that dwelleth in the secret place of the Most High shall abide under the shadow of the Almighty." We have access thither, not by any merit of ours, or because we are baptised or vaccinated or keep Lent, but because we are saved by the grace of God, and have right to go into the immediate presence of God. The thing about it that is amazing to me is that I can *enjoy* it. Angels veil their faces, but I can look on God and live. It means access into the place of the absolute holiness. How precious the Blood of Jesus is! how wonderful the work of the Holy Spirit, taking the like of you and me and making us so that we can have not only access, but acceptance and enjoyment when we get right in!

Supposing the Lord said He was going to deny access for a month. There would be a queer run then, at the end of the month, to the throne of grace. Yet He leaves that way open for every born-again one.

Supposing I had the right to go to Buckingham

Palace, immediately I made to go in I would be asked, " Where are you going? " I would say, " I am a privileged man, I am going in there," and I would be told, " Man, Nicholson, you're a boy! "

When I was working as an Evangelist in one city, I got acquainted with a wealthy man who said to me one day, " Whenever you want me, there is a key to get in by that private door whenever you like." He was a very busy man, making a lot of money; and, he not having the time to spend it, some of us did the spending of it for him. One day, when I was coming out of his room, a man I knew said to me, " What were you doing in there? I would give £10 for every minute you spend in there." At that rate, twenty minutes' time there would be worth £200! That was great.

But do you know anything about your privilege of access to God? King George could not help you very far to access into the presence of God Almighty, with whom nothing is impossible. What a privilege to have!

Suppose you had the privilege of taking whatever you liked in a big warehouse, and you came out with only a pocket handkerchief in your hand. You would be called a fool. And yet that is how many people treat their privilege of access to God. What do you come out with when you get to God? Remember, it is written, " Whatsoever you shall ask in My name I will do." Many are living half-starved and poverty-stricken lives, in spiritual beggary, and yet all these resources are at their disposal. May the Lord help us to rise to our privileges.

We have access to God with unveiled faces. You can tell by the way some people pray whether they have access or not. If a man asked his wife for his porridge in the way in which some ministers pray, she would throw the pot at him. Is the grass growing on that path? or are you using it, and are you having face to face fellowship with your Father?

(3) We have the privilege of *communion with the Lord.*

Some people would not want to go the length of their foot with me. They would say, "I would not be seen with that man,"—and maybe the feeling is mutual! But I walk with the Lord and He with me. We can do without the other crowd. If I got the best people to walk with me, and lost communion with God, would it be worth it?

A man said to me once, "Nicholson, I would like to be your friend, and I want you to do what I tell you." I said, "I could not pay the price." He said, "It will cost you far more not to do it," and I replied, "No, it would cost me too much, it would cost me my walk with God. I have walked twenty-five years with Jesus, and I would not go back on Him, I would not change for anyone."

Woman, He is with you when you are washing the kitchen floor. When you are worried about next week's rent, and wonder where it is to come from, He is with you. Do you take advantage of the privilege? Do you walk with Jesus? Enoch walked with God and kept his feet on the ground; I know that, because he had sons and daughters. I do not know anyone in the world that I know better than the Lord. I do not know my wife or my mother the way I know the Lord. I do not know the best friends I ever had the way I know the Lord. We walk together, my Lord and I, because we are in fellowship, and there is nothing that I have but is His. All my sins were made His one day, and all my joys are His now. Glory to God, we laugh together.

I was golfing one Monday morning with some friends, and on reaching a certain point I said, "Here is an opportunity to have a good time with the Lord."

One of them said, "I do not mix my golf with religion. Could you pray while you were at golf?"

I said, "If I could not pray in the middle of golf, I would not golf."

If I could not pray in the middle of a laugh or joke I would not laugh again. But Jesus enters into all my sorrows and joys. There is not a burden that He does not bear, and, thank God, there is nothing He has that I have not. If I am his, everything He has is mine. It is said that Rockefeller has more than a billion of money. Well, there has not been a billion minutes since Jesus was born up to this minute, and yet Rockefeller has all this. Supposing that this billionaire said, "Everything I have got is yours, help yourself."

Sister, you have got such a one as that with you, and yet you have a face so long that it is away down about your feet. This is a life of intimate fellowship, sharing each other's feelings.

(4) We have the privilege of *His name*. Did you ever give anybody your name? I am always away from home; and every time, before I go away, I have to sign a big document, giving a fellow power to use my name to look after the children and the house, and he signs my name. It is a queer risk! But the Lord has taken that risk, and He says, "Nicholson, here is My name, just go into the bank and get what you want."

Yet many are saying, " Lord, do You think You can afford to give me a penny? Lord, I would like a shilling or two, but I am afraid I would be asking too much." " *Whatsoever* you shall ask in My name, that will I do "—why?—" that the Father may be glorified in the Son." The glory of God is in the name, and the using of it, and He is giving you the use of His name. I say at the Throne of Grace " In the name of Jesus, here is my need." Supposing I go to the banker of our friend Mr Montgomery* and say, " Would you give me £20 for the sake of Mr Montgomery? " he would be whistling for the police. But supposing Mr Montgomery gives me a cheque for that amount, I get it at once.

Seven times before Jesus died, in His talk in the Upper Room in the course of His farewell address He said, " In My name." " I am giving you the use of My name." This is the " name above every name."

(5) We have the privilege of *service*. Imagine serving the Lord. I have never apologised for my job. I am sorry for the way I do it, but I have never been sorry about the way Jesus has treated me. I have had a three-fold ordination—ordained to eternal life, ordained to bring forth fruit, ordained by Presbytery. Never hang your head; put your head up and straighten your back. You are in a grand service. When you get to Heaven He will not look to see how many academical degrees you have got, but He will look to see how many scars you have got, and find out how many jobs you took.

* Merchant in Bangor, and local leader of the Christian Workers' Union, a brother of Rev. Dr. Henry Montgomery of Belfast.

(6) We have the privilege of *reigning with Him,* right here and now. The Bible speaks of " reigning in life." Some people just exist. Their whole biography might be summed up in three words,—born, married, died. There are very few monarchs in the world, but, glory to God, I am one of them! We are looking at our foes and enemies, monarchs of all. The Crowning Day is coming. I am going to reign with Christ, not merely to be reigned over by Him, but to reign with Him. We are to be priests and kings. It is your privilege to enjoy this now.

Are we living up to our privileges? Do men look at us with a tug at their heart and say, " I wish I was like him " or, " What a Saviour that woman has! That is a great salvation." Is that so? Well, it is your privilege and mine. How many bring an evil report from the good land, and men and women turn away saying, " If that is the half-starved beggarly thing salvation is, we'll have none of it." But if we are enjoying our privileges, how the world will sit up and take note, and long to have them too.

In The Song of Solomon, you remember, the representatives of the king got this country maid into the harem of the old voluptuous king, the wisest man and the biggest fool that ever lived. She was a slave, but she began to tell about her country lover, and she described him until those who heard her said, " Where is thy beloved, that we may seek him too." Is that the way people think about you and me? God grant it! Amen.

3
The Christian's Perfection

A child does not forsake the alphabet, but he goes on. We are not to forsake the principles of the doctrines of Christ, but we are to advance from them and go right on. We are not to be always bothering about the foundations, always practising scales.

There is a great deal of haziness regarding this matter of Christian perfection, but there is no haziness in the Word of God. It is clear and simple that everyone born of the Spirit is called to perfection. Instead of being scared of becoming perfect, we should have it as the longing of our hearts.

This perfection which the Word of God teaches is not absolute perfection: absolute perfection belongs to God alone. It does not mean that you and I are sinless. There never will be a time, until we awake in His likeness, when we are "saved to sin no more." But we are going on towards that final perfection promised. There is a sense in the Word of God where we have absolute perfection.

(1) I would say, we have it in our Saviour, an absolutely perfect Saviour. There is no flaw in Him. People say, "I would like to be saved, but there are so many hypocrites." Forget all about them, and be taken up with the Saviour. Neither sacrament, cere-

mony, pope nor priest can add to salvation. We have an absolutely perfect Saviour, and perfect access to God. The veil has been rent from the top to the bottom; and, while the Church has been trying to sew it up, and to say you and I have no right except to go in through *them,* we have a perfect right to this access.

(2) We have perfection in *forgiveness.* When God forgives, He does it like God. When I forgive I can never forget. I may freely forgive you, but every time I recall your name I may remember the injury that I did you or that you did me. But when God forgives He forgets: He remembers our sins no more for ever.

(3) We have absolutely perfect *security.* I am not only saved in Christ, but I am safe in Christ. My Saviour will never be in glory and leave me behind. Why? Because I am a part of His body, and He will never have a maimed body; I am part of His bride, and He will never have a divorce. It is an indissoluble union.

(4) We have perfect *guidance.* They that are the sons of God are led by the Spirit of God.

In these senses, then, there is absolute perfection. But we can never, while here, claim for ourselves a perfection that is final. There is the danger of making too little of Christian perfection, a common danger in the Church. There is an ignoring of it altogether, a disbelief in the possibility of it, or an absolute denial of it. Some almost talk as if it were a good thing to have a little sin remaining about us, to humble and sanctify us. But sin is not sent to sanctify men. God is the enemy of sin, and it never did any man or woman any good. There is the danger of making too little of perfection.

The other side of it is that we may make too much of it, and take up an untenable position by going the length of saying that evil is absolutely eradicated. I know of a man who said he had not sinned for seventeen years, and that he was just as perfect as Jesus was on earth. If that is a possibility, if that is God's way of doing business, I am a candidate for it. I hate sin with all the passion of my heart. I have no sympathy with it, and make no allowance for it. Yet day after day I pray "Forgive us our trespasses." If we take up an untenable position, the devil gets advantage over us and it leads to back-sliding.

Then there is the danger of using unscriptural terms regarding the teaching. The Bible has a peculiar way of handling words. I have a vocabulary peculiar to myself, and my friend Mr Govan* has one peculiar to him: if you want to understand us, you must understand our vocabulary. In the same way, if you want to understand the vocabulary of the Bible, you must get the Word of God and see what is involved in any specific statement in it. The word "destroy" is used in the part of scripture where a woman is spoken of as being loosed from her husband; it means that you and I are loosed from sin, but it does not mean that the devil and sin are destroyed.

There is a lot said about the law of gravity, and the main principle of it is that it attracts everything to the earth. It is only fools and theological professors that

*Mr. J. G. Govan, President of the Faith Mission, who was leading the meetings at which the addresses were given.

talk about things falling *up;* everything in God's world falls *down.* But if you hold up your arm, the law of life in its sets it free for the time being from the law of gravity. It does not suppress or destroy the law of gravity, but it counteracts it. A greater law than the law of gravity is the law of life in the arm. It is the same with us in Christ: I am only free from sin as I abide in Christ, and daily and hourly abandon myself to Him. Mr Moody said one day when he was in Scotland, "After nearly thirty years of serving God, and building up a Christian character, I might go out of this church and in ten minutes' time commit a crime that would wreck those fifty years of Christian character and testimony." We all know the possibility of it. Our only security is in a constant abiding in Christ.

The perfection taught in the Word of God is not the perfection of *finality,* but of *condition.* If you say to a mother, "What a bonny baby you have! Is that a perfect baby?" she replies, "Why, certainly, it is a perfect baby." Yet that baby has not reached finality: it grows apace; it daily forgets the things that are past and goes right on to maturity. That is the perfection taught in the Bible,—the perfection of condition, not of consummation. Would you expect as much from a convert three weeks old as from a Christian walking in the will of God for fifteen years? Yet that young convert may be as perfect in the sight of God, at his stage, as that other who is fifteen years farther on. Springtime is all around, and you see the buds coming out on the branches. You ask "Is that a perfect bud?" Certainly, but you watch every day and find that the bud is forgetting the things that are past and pressing on till ripe and luscious fruit will be the perfection of finality.

Again, people are scared because they confound infirmity and sin. It is a very delicate difference, and it is dangerous trying to show the difference. You may know the difference between imperfection and sin. Before I understood it I was in a fix about it. Sin is a voluntary transgression of the law; infirmity is an involuntary transgression of the law. The one is deliberate and wilful and the other may be a spontaneous thing, the outcome of wrong judgment or ignorance or weakness on your part or mine in an unguarded moment. Sin always breaks your communion with God, but infirmity never does. You have the word "faultless" in the Testament, and the word "blameless"; you will never be *faultless* till you stand in the presence of God, but you may be *blameless.* We are to be "blameless and harmless, children of God."

A lady was always fond of putting her boots on the fender to warm before putting them on. Her little girl tried to improve on this practice and put them in the oven. When the mother wanted them she could not find them; and then she turned and said to her little girl, "Did you see Mamma's boots?" She said, "Oh yes, I wanted them nice and warm for you, and I put them in the oven." When the mother opened the oven door she saw nothing but smoke and ashes. Was the child faultless? No, but the child was blameless. In its will and intention it desired to please its mother. That is the perfection the Bible desires and demands, and can work in you and me. We may make varieties of mistakes, but we may be blameless and harmless all the same. One of the laws of Great

Britain is a law called the Crimes Prevention Act. Supposing I was a noted burglar, and they caught me under suspicious circumstances at night. The policeman spotted me and apprehended me. He took me to the jail, and when I stood before the judge, the judge asked—" Did that man actually burgle the house?" The answer given was " No, but he is a noted burglar and we caught him under suspicious circumstances, and we believed he was there with no good intention." The judge passes sentence on me because I was there to do it, going to commit the crime. So they have the Crimes Prevention Act; they take the will for the deed in the eyes of the law. Many a time I have tried to run a mission for the Lord, and people have said hard things about me; but they have never said half of the hard things about me that I have said about myself. Many a time I have tried to preach and only made a mug of it. God knows I have tried, and He takes the will for the deed. The easiest one to please is the Lord; He knows the motive, and He can see back into the soul. The world judges us by our actions. People say about me, " My, that man is unfit to preach and should not be allowed in a pulpit"; but God knows I desire to serve Him, and so He winks at a whole lot of stuff that you do not understand. The hardest thing under heaven is to please fifty people, and the easiest thing is to please one, and that is God. You have only one to bother about then.

When I was in business in Belfast for a while, and used to travel up in the train, many of us did not bother about our tickets; and every now and then they had a periodical inspection. When we had left our tickets in another jacket there was a lot of growling.

A man said to the collector one day, " You are not very popular here," and he replied, " Oh, well, it does not concern me, there is the manager there that I am trying to please." If you begin to please the Lord you may make mistakes, but the Lord knows you want to please Him. Your judgment, and mine, is not perfect; no man's is. Many a time we do things that we mean to be right, and we try to please God; but because of the infirmity of our judgment we make a mug of it.

You remember the story of the Christian barber who was busy stropping his razor one day when he was about to shave a customer, and he said to the customer, " Are you ready to die? " We smile at that, but all the same the barber was trying to help that man, and no doubt he would learn a bit better after a while. Do you mean to tell me that God will judge that barber the way the customer did? Did that barber try to please his Lord? Certainly, and God will reward him for it while you and I may laugh at his blundering mistake. Outsiders do not see that we are trying to please God, but God knows it. They only see the blundering mistakes you and I make because of the infirmity of our judgment.

Now let us consider what the Word of God says a perfect Christian is. The word " perfect " is used in various places, and in various ways, in the New Testament, and every time it is used it is translated perfect, but in the original it has not altogether that meaning.

(1) 2 Cor. xiii., 9: " This also we wish, even your perfection." Verse 11, " Finally, brethren, farewell. Be perfect, be of good comfort." 1 Cor. i., 10, and Eph. iv., 12, " He gave some apostles and evangelists,

some pastors and teachers—" What for?—" for the perfecting of the saints, the work of the ministry, the edifying of the body of Christ." The word used in these scriptures is the word " adjust." He gave to the Church evangelists and teachers for the adjustment of the saints. The perfect Christian is a man who may be making mistakes, but he is perfectly adjusted to Christ. My right hand is very imperfect, and when I write I write with my second finger. My hand is not even as clean as it might be, but when my head wishes that hand to do anything it does it. I can move my hand in any direction, but all the same it is very imperfect. It is all mutilated, and not as clean as it might be, but anything the head wants it to do it is right there. I have never heard that right hand say to me, " Well, Willie, I am kind of tired, I will not bother you when you want me." When I used to serve the devil I never had that right hand say, " Oh, you would not like to hit that fellow." Mind you, that hand has gone up and down to my mouth a queer lot of times, as I have been sticking the stuff down that hole under my nose. If it had belonged to the union it would have been out on strike long ago! I do not care, day or night, where I am or how I am, that right hand is doing its duty, though it is not a perfect hand. I have watched doctors operating by the hundred; and I have noticed that, before a doctor begins operating, he washes vigorously, and by and by dips his hands into a basin of microchloric. My hand is all impaired, but it is perfect, perfectly adjusted to my head. Whatever my head wants that hand to do, it is right there. The backs of that Bible I hold in my hand are not perfect; I am not a book-binder, but I can see flaws in the binding. At the same time, it is adjusted to the book. My watch is not altogether perfect, but its wheels are adjusted to keep the time, and its hands are adjusted to show me the time. As a minister and evangelist I am very imperfect, but I defy any man or devil to say that I am not adjusted. If I am not adjusted to the mind of God at this moment, it is not because I refuse. As far as I know at this moment, my will is the will of my God, and I desire to please Him. "He gave unto the Church apostles . . for the adjustment of the saints." Our adjustment is not only to Christ, the Head, but to every other member of the Body of Christ. Here is my imperfect hand, but it never said, "I am not going to do anything because I am not your eye or your nose. I am not going to do anything because I am not your foot. If I was only the left hand instead of the right hand I would do something, but because I am the right hand I am out on strike." It never did that. The same with the eye. Every member of the body is a contributing and distributing member. The perfect Christian is one who is adjusted to Christ, the Head, and to every other member. I cannot play an organ, but you can. All the notes in the hymn book are to me like swallows on a telegraph wire. Some of you women can nurse, but, God bless me, I could not do it. Some of you can sing, but I cannot. I could not make a pair of boots or a batch of bread. I could not make a suit of clothes, but I can wear them. I could not cut my hair, but I can shave myself. I need you to bake the bread as much as you need me to preach the gospel.

Our servant girl was just as good as any member of the family at home, but our position was different. I noticed Mary's face one morning at prayers, and at the finish I said to her, "It will be a queer eye-opener to you when you get to the judgment seat." "How is that?" she asked. "There will be dozens of people over this world who will say 'Thank God for Mary.'" By this time her eyes were opening, and her mouth as well, and she said to me, "You are not making a fool of me?" I said, "No," and I went on: "I could clean my boots as well as you, and I could cook a meal in some kind of way; I might attend the door as well as you, but how long would I then get to pray or to study? You will get the reward on the Great Day because you have given me the opportunity to get alone with God's Word."

A miner once said to me, "I don't believe in a paid preacher; I don't believe in any man getting paid for preaching." I said, "It is a dirty shame." He said, "Well, aren't you getting paid for preaching?" and I said, "I certainly am not." "But," he said, "you get paid." I said, "I do, but not for preaching." "What do you get paid for?" and I replied, "To keep me while preaching." I said, "What do you do?" and he replied, "I am a coal miner." "You are saved, aren't you?" and he said, "Yes." "What do you work for?" At that time, he said, it was about £3 10s a week. "I don't believe in a miner working for money at all," I replied, and he said, "I never heard the like of that." I said, "Listen! You are a minister of the goodness of God, and I am a minister of the grace of God. That is the only difference; and if I am preaching for money, and you are howking coals for money, we are both alike; but if you are howking coal for the glory of God, to warm the bodies of God's people, your money is only an incidental thing to keep you at the job. It is exactly the same with preaching." He said, "I never thought of that."

I am trying to pour out my love and knowledge upon you, and you are pouring out your money upon me. I get your money and you get what I know of God's Word. When you get a perfect Christian, we are all adjusted to every other member of the body. Some of you will get a queer eye-opener when you get to heaven! The perfect Christian, says the Word of God, is one who is adjusted to the Head and to every member of the body.

(2) 1 Thess. v., 23: "I pray God your whole spirit, soul, and body be preserved blameless"; also James i., 4: The word there is the word "complete"; I am adjusted to the Lord to be complete. I am adjusted to my fellow-believer to be complete and entire, wanting nothing. If you can sing, sing. If you have executive ability, give it. If you have got preaching ability, don't be stingy with it! If I have got the knowledge of God, I empty myself every time. If you have got money, don't be a miser.

Suppose my eyes were to say, "All right, we are adjusted to the head, but the right one will not look." Suppose my two jaws were to say, "Well, we are adjusted to the head, but the lower one won't move." Isn't it that way many a time? People are adjusted in the mind but not in the pocket. They are adjusted with one thing, but not with another. There is not a complete adjustment; they say, "Lord, I will give You my Sunday, but I will do as I like on Monday, Tuesday and Wednesday." "Lord, I will keep Lent, but I will give the devil the rest of the year." "Lord, I will serve You in the Sunday School, but don't touch my money."

"Lord, I will serve You, but don't touch my time, I am going to do with my time as I like." But in our adjustment as perfect Christians we are not only to be complete to the Head but complete to each other. Whatever you have, it is all necessary for the perfecting of the body, the perfecting of the saints.

(3) Another word, Ephesians iv., 13: "Unto a perfect man, unto the measure of the stature of the fulness of Christ." Hebrews vi., 1, "Let us go on to maturity, perfection." The word there is the word "Maturity."

How many men and women are just overgrown babies! Something has .arrested their development. They are twenty or thirty years in Christ, but they are nothing but big babies. Instead of the church being an armoury for drilling, it is a nursery, and the minister is a wet nurse, and every Sunday he has a bottle with a wee teat. They can sing, "Like a mighty army moves the Church of God," "Onward Christian Soldiers, marching as to war," but they are babies all the same. Instead of taking 16-inch guns, we have a whole lot of go-carts with big babies. Instead of gun-carriages and ammunition carriages it is baby carriages.

You know there are some outstanding peculiarities in a baby. You can always tell a baby, in the first instance, by this, that it cannot help itself. Did you ever know anything so helpless as a wee baby? Did you ever know more helpless creatures in the church, sitting in the pew for years and not able to help themselves to a decent meal out of God's Word? All they know is just by the minister doing what their mothers used to do with them when they were children, crumble the bread for them. Whenever the minister gives you a wee bit of strong meat, you are like a child; you begin to boof. You say, "I did not like that preaching to-day." Whenever we begin to talk of the second blessing, and sanctification, they are like to vomit it up. They have been used to the milk so long that when you put a bit of meat in their mouth they squirm.

Another thing is that a baby cannot help anybody else. Put an anxious soul beside some of you, and it would put cold chills down your back. If anybody was dying you could not go and help them. I know a lot of ministers like that. I said to a friend of mine, "I wish you would look over your pulpit and say—'If anybody would like to be converted, come round at the close of the service!'" He could only give a card of decision, and ask them to sign it.

You can always tell a baby, also, because it is very touchy. When I would speak sternly to my children the holy water would begin to come to their eyes, and their chin would move. We find people saying, "I did not like that sermon. I will not go back again," and they are in the corner with their finger in their mouth. Says the Lord Jesus Christ, "We have played the music and you won't dance, we have mourned and you won't weep; what are we to do with you?" "I don't like that man's meetings, he is laughing and carrying-on all the time." "I don't like the church because it is so dry and dead." What on earth *do* you like, you big baby? Again, you can always tell a baby because it is ignorant, it doesn't know B from a bull's foot. It catches hold of its wee toe and looks at it. It puts everything towards its mouth. Do you know any big babies, ignorant of the Bible doctrines of grace and what their church stands for? Some say, "You should not make them laugh." But ninety per cent. of my audiences are babies. If I was to stand solemnly in the pulpit you would say, " That is dry, it is dead "; so I have to tickle you and keep you in good humour, and all the time you are laughing and feeling good I am jagging at you and getting something down. When a minister gets his nose on the paper to read his sermon, people begin to dose.

The Lord does not want us to be babies. We are to leave the principles of the doctrines and go on to maturity, to full stature.

(4) 2 Timothy iii., 17 : " That the man of God may be perfect, thoroughly furnished unto every good work." Hebrews xiii., 31 : " The God of peace make you perfect in every good work." The word " perfect " is the word " ready." What is the perfect Christian? It is the man adjusted to the Head and every member of the body. The adjustment is complete, there are no reservations in the surrender, the completeness and adjustment is going on to maturity. Might I be guilty of a grammatical mistake? We are completer to-morrow, better adjusted to-morrow, more fully adjusted to-morrow, and all the time we are " ready for every good work." When the Boer War broke out, two or three drunken generals were sent out to make a mess of things; and when they saw things going hard against the British, they sent over to Lord Roberts saying, " Will you take charge of the Expeditionary Force in South Africa? " The reply was, " Yes, I will." " When will you be ready to leave? " and he said, " I have been ready for fifteen years." He saw that, after the Basuto War, things should have been cleaned up then.

" I want you to teach in the Sunday School," and you

should be ready to say, "I am your boy." "I would like you to give your testimony," and the reply should be, "All right, I will do it." "Can you help us in that meeting or hall?" "I am ready."

I ask you,—Are you a perfect Christian, entirely surrendered to your Lord, complete and entire in the surrender, going on more and more surrendering day by day, going on to maturity; and not only that, but ready all the time for every call and demand and command of your Lord? Thank God, this is the word, "He that hath begun a good work in you will perpetuate and perfect that work till the day of Christ." Give Him a chance, and He will perfect you now as to condition, and you will go on to perfection's sacred height.

4

The Christian's Peace

Of all the personal letters Paul wrote, that to the Philippians is the only one where there is no word of condemnation. They are all words of commendation. There never was any trouble in that church except with a couple of old maids, who were like a couple of Kilkenny cats with their tails tied together hanging over a clothes line. Now see what he says in ch. iv., v. 11: "I have learned . . . everywhere and in all things I possess the secret both to be full and to be hungry. . . . I can do"—*some* things?—No, "I can do *all* things,"—all things but give up tobacco? All things but govern myself? All things but control my tongue? All things but, but, but— "Wonderful Jesus! Wonderful Saviour! I can do all things. "But," you say, "I cannot testify in the open air. I am not built that way. I was not brought up that way."

No, but this is something you *can* do *in Christ.* "I can do all things through Him that strengtheneth me."

I once conducted a mission in a Baptist Church; but, when the communion came round, I was not allowed to sit at the table, because I was a Presbyterian and not a Baptist. So there are *some* things I cannot do!

But it is of the Christian's Peace that I want to speak to you now. In the midst of our perils and perplexities, and in spite of our imperfections, we have peace. Some people hardly believe it, but there is a peace in the saved, sanctified life that the world knows nothing of. Let us look at it together.

There are two kinds of peace mentioned in the New Testament. The first peace, for blood-washed men and women, is—" Justified by faith, we have peace with God." That is not something that you gain: it is a gift. It is not a payment. The moment you believe, the Lord gives you peace. It does not matter what your denomination may be, or whether you have any denomination, or who you are or what you are, if you are saved by God's grace you have peace with God through our Lord Jesus Christ.

But there is another peace mentioned in Scripture, which you find here in Phil. iv., 7—" the peace of God, to garrison your heart and mind in Christ Jesus." Every born-again one has peace *with* God, but it is not every born-again one that has the peace *of* God, though he *should* have it. The first peace is determined by your union with the Lord; the second, by your communion with your Lord. If I am walking in the light as He is in the light, we are having fellowship one with another and I possess the peace of God. " Come unto Me . . . and I will give you rest." This is a first call. But beyond it there is something far richer and deeper. " There remaineth a rest for the people of God," and they who enter into this rest have ceased from their own works, and enter into a possession that is peculiar and wonderfully precious,—the peace of God. Now—

(1) Consider the *nature* of this peace. It is called a peace that " passeth all understanding." You cannot understand it, nor can I. It is no good trying to. You may be an M.A., a B.D., a K.G., and an X.Y.Z.; you may be the wisest man that ever lived; but you cannot understand this peace. I can understand the peace that comes after you have been sick and have got well; the peace that comes when you have been up against some tragedy in life and now it is past; the peace that comes to a business man after he has gone through a financial crisis and gets his feet on the ground again; but this peace of God is beyond my understanding.

I was once in lodgings where there was only one little boy of six years. One Saturday afternoon he came in saying, " Oh, my head! I have such a sore head." Before the night was over he was unconscious, and he died of tubercular meningitis. He was their only child. The mother never let him out of her arms. Neighbours offered help, but she held on to the child. When the breath had left the wee body they said, " Give it to us, we will dress it." No, she dressed it herself. When the funeral came, she watched the procession making its way from the door; then she went back to her bed and slept twenty-four hours of unbroken sleep, after which she got up and went back to her work.

Some who did not know any better said, " Tell me, did you love your boy? "

" Does a mother love her only child? Do fish swim? Do birds fly? "

" Why were you not in hysterics like the others? Why did you not cry with inconsolable grief? "

The peace of God, that passeth all understanding, had guarded her heart and mind. I preached for six weeks in that town, but that sermon of hers did more than all the six weeks' preaching.

What did you do when you got into sorrow? What an amount of tearing of hair and hysterics was there! What an amount of dope the doctor had to stick in you! In China they sing and dress themselves in white at a funeral. You and I start to mourn and put black on, and yet they have a heathen religion and we have Christianity.

A friend of mine in Glasgow lived down in Ayrshire, in a beautiful mansion with twenty-five acres round it. He was an out-and-out godly man. One day he was sitting at his breakfast table with the family, reading his correspondence. They had their morning prayer after breakfast, as if nothing had occurred. But, after the children left, he passed a letter to his wife containing the news that every penny they had was gone.

"Well, dear," she said, "we have each other, and, above all, we have CHRIST."

They are now in two rooms and kitchen in Glasgow, working for their meat.

Understand it? No, you cannot understand it. In the midst of persecution and opposition, malignity and irritation, one can have this peace. Have you got it? Not only is it incomprehensible in its nature, but it is the peace of a quiet heart. There is no flurry, no tear and wear, no fuss. It is awfully nice to come in contact with people who have a quiet heart. The heart is at rest, with not a flutter or struggle, not a moment's dread or fear of past, present, or future. There is not only a quiet heart, but a quiet conscience, having no fear of God (in the sense of *slavish* fear), because their sins are buried under the blood. That is the nature of it. The sin question between them and God is settled for ever; there is nothing controversial between them and their Saviour.

And it is the peace of a surrendered will. Their delight, day in and day out, is " Not my will, but Thine, be done." Jock Troup was singing to us lately of the " sweet beloved will of God." That is mere poetry and sentiment to a whole lot of people; but when you come into this peace you enter into a surrender that is the luxury of life, the delight of the heart. It rejoices you to think that Christ would take the like of you up; it is a glorious place, and a joyful experience, to live day in and day out in God's will.

Not only that, but it is the peace of a calm spirit. There is a calmness and quietness amidst all the rush of life. On the ocean surface billows are roaring and surging, but twenty-five fathoms down the sea is like an eternal calm. Wonderful peace! It is " the gift of God's love."

But it is also the peace of a happy service. You are quite free to help others. How many there are to-day so full of unrest and dispeace that they have no time to help another. Many a man and woman, finding their satisfaction in money, surroundings, and friends, has a better peace than some of you have found in Jesus Christ. When you would tell them something of what you have, they have something better than you. But there is a place in Christ where you can have this peace that passeth all understanding.

How many are so full of worry, care, and anxiety! Take up your Bible and study what God did with worrying people, murmuring people, and you will get a surprise. Whenever you begin to worry or murmur at

God, you are charging God's love and will and power. It is a great sin to worry while professing to be in Christ. Thank God, there is a place in Christ where there is "not a shade of worry, not a blast of care," and where all these things are like water on a duck's back. There you have the peace that passeth all understanding, so that you are free to start and serve and help others instead of being merely taken up with your own cares. It is a peace that you cannot understand, but it is also a peace that you cannot misunderstand. Any man or woman who has it will be willing for anything, anywhere.

I have heard some good preachers, but I could not help saying to myself there was something wanting. Moody was one of the greatest preachers in Chicago, and at the beginning of his preaching four old women used to pray for him. This nettled him, and he said, "Why do you pray for me?" They replied, "Because there is something you need." And their prayers were answered. He came into the experience of that second rest, and God got full possession of him, and he had "the peace of God." Glory to God! There is a fellowship in the Christian life like that of the three disciples among the eleven. (Matt. xxvi., 36, 37.) They are up against Christ closer than the other eight. Are you amongst those that I have been trying to describe?

(2) What is the *source* of this peace? "The God of peace be with you always." Seven times in the New Testament you have that expression used about God being the author of peace. You can get peace nowhere else except from Him. There is eternal calm in the

Divine Nature: you never get Him worried or flurried. And, just as surely as it is in God, it may be in you and me. We may know it as ours if we are only willing to pay the price for this peace that is peculiarly God's peace. You cannot divorce it from God. You can take away my money, and yet leave *me;* but you could not take away the fragrance of the rose and leave the rose; you could not take away the bird and leave the song. You could not take the peace away from God and still have God. It is all of God; it is only from God we receive it. When you and I dwell in the secret place of the Lord, and know that inner calm and peace, we know it belongs to Him.

(3) What is the *channel* of peace? How does He convey it to us?

2 Thess., iii., 16. "Now the Lord of peace Himself"—why do they need to put that in? Because the Spirit of God wants to emphasise that you cannot divorce the peace from the Lord—"the Lord of peace Himself give you peace always." How? "*By all means.*" It is not some kind of thing that gets you up in the clouds, when you forget all about washing pots and scrubbing floors.

A business man in America was answering a telephone call in my presence one day. I gathered, from what was said, that it had to do with the appointment of a committee; and one remark he made was—"Yes, I would appoint so-and-so, because, he is a man of vision, while he keeps both feet on the ground." That's the right position.

Some women forget about the cinders in the grate, and when they are washing the hall forget to lift the mats. This peace comes to us along practical lines. "My peace I give unto you, not as the world giveth." How does the world give? "I will give you more pay and less hours of work, take away your sickness and danger, and do away with your trials and temptations, and you will get peace."

I knew an old fellow who was hypochondriacal, with more money than sense, and he thought every disease and sickness was coming to him. One day he thought he was dying—and they would have been glad if he had! The doctor advised a trip to the Continent, but he came back just as bad as he was. The doctor said to him,—"You want to get out of yourself."

"Man, doctor, how could you get out of yourself?"

That's the rub. "The Lord . . . give you peace *by all means.*" Sister, although your body may be racked with pain and suffering, you can have the peace of God. Although you may be living in a home that is a hell upon earth, with a drunken husband, you can have the peace of God. Although you may be working amongst the most ungodly gang, you can have this peace. And, glory to God, it will be richer the harder your circumstances are. The easier your life and mine is, the less we know about it; but the harder the life is the richer it is. I have learned more on a sickbed than ever I did in a pulpit. I learned more when I was being kicked up and down the country than at any other time. We are wanting to get rid of the trouble, and the Lord says, "I will keep you *in* the trouble," and He will give you something to glory in while in it.

I remember one of the week-night prayer meetings in an old church in Bangor, at which the late Mr McLachlan was present after he had lost his wife. A telegram had now come with a message that his boy had been killed in the Boer War; and he stood up in that meeting and said, " Dear friends, I want you to pray for me. Don't pray that I may *bear* this sorrow, but that I may *glory in* it." Did you ever get there?

I buried the body of a dear old saint who had walked with her husband on the road to Heaven for fifty-six years. When she passed away to meet the Lord the husband said to me, " Mind you, after living and loving during all these years, if it would not be misunderstood, I could shout and praise and magnify God that Maggie's Crowning Day has come; but it might be misunderstood." One Christian widow knelt at the grave of her husband and said, " Blessed Jesus, I thank Thee for fifteen years of heaven on earth."

Yes, it comes " by all means," whether in joy or in sorrow, in tribulation or trial, in poverty or adversity, in work or out of it. It does not matter what your circumstances may be, you have something that will meet your need. Would it not be a testimony for God if every one of us who are saved by His grace would enter into this peace, the peace of God? In the midst of all the varying vicissitudes of life, by all means, this peace comes. It is fine.

Is it some kind of sentimental idea to you? or is it a real experience in your heart and life? Do you know it? Have you entered into this secret and learned it? Do you possess it amidst all the varieties of experiences, flowing like a river upon your own soul and through your life in benediction and blessing to others?

(4) How long will it last?

That is a queer question. When you and I got peace

with God through our Lord Jesus Christ, they gave us about a month or six weeks; but the Lord gave us eternal life. How long will that peace last? For ever. How long will the peace of God last? Just as long as you like; not one minute longer than you like, and not one minute shorter than you like. The moment I doubt the providences of God my peace vanishes. The moment I disobey the will of God my peace vanishes. When you begin to question the experiences of life, when you begin to whine and groan, your peace goes. When you take everything from His dear Hand, whether you are in persecution or sickness, trial, temptation, joy, pain, sorrow, adversity, poverty, riches, everything from His dear Hand, the peace abides. When you begin to look at the second causes, the means through which God's providences come to you, and to quibble and quarrel with the way God brings them about, this peace vanishes. This peace of God goes when we ask—" Why should I be sick? why am I laid on my bed? why did I get kicked out of a job? why am I on the dole?" But when you look up and say, " Lord, I thank You for every touch of pain, every moment of joy, every day of prosperity," when you thank God that your nose is up against the grindstone, your peace abides. When you begin to disobey what you know God's will to be, good-bye to your peace. If He wants you for active service, or to give your money, if He wants you in any place or way, and there is rebellion against His will, good-bye to peace. So it just lasts as long as you like: as long as you want it, it is at your disposal. The Lord " by all means " gives us peace, but not one moment longer than we like. The Lord will not force it upon us.

(5) How does this peace become ours? It is great to talk about all these beautiful things regarding it, but is it for us?

Yes! "*My* peace I give unto you," the Lord said—it is a thing peculiarly His—"I give unto you, not as the world giveth give I unto you." You cannot buy it, you cannot pay any money for it. It is beyond all reckoning. You never merit or deserve it. You may suffer pain or torture in your body, you may give every penny you have to feed the poor, you may go under all kinds of mutilations; but you cannot get peace in that way. God is too big to *sell* it to you, but He is so big that He *gives* it. "My peace I give unto you." If you are willing to receive it from Him, to say, "Lord Jesus, I yield me to be Thine, all I have and am I yield to Thee, Lord I receive this blessing—Thy peace, the peace of God that passeth all understanding, to guard and garrison heart and mind," then it is yours.

Mother, you have perhaps felt, as we have talked of these things together, that it has been like peace on earth; but you are going back into a cold world and perhaps a dead church. You feel inclined to say, "My! my! I wish I could stay here and be in this atmosphere; Jesus, let us build three tabernacles up here."

"Oh, no, I want you down there to cast out devils. My peace I give you."

Dear tired mother with aching heart, brother in business, wearied and tired, puzzled and wondering how long this crisis is going to last because you are up against it and full of care, to *you* Jesus says, "My peace I give, I give, I give." You can have it to-day, and all through the varied experiences of life. And then, when it comes to the end of the journey and the end of the day, thank God, that peace that passeth all understanding will still garrison the heart and mind.

When I was in the Lanarkshire Christian Union, in Scotland, there was a dear sister called Miss Jack, a long, lanky, stretched-out sort of woman. She did the visiting, and helped a lot. But she was a terror!—a constant rebuke, and a constant inspiration. When she died, it was of tuberculosis, and her body was emaciated, and for days there was hardly a breath in her body. As they sat up with her, it seemed as if every particle of life was gone. They saw her lips moving, and on leaning over her they heard the words,

> "There's a deep, settled peace in my soul;
> There's a deep, settled peace in my soul;
> Though the billows of death near me roll,
> He abides, CHRIST abides!"

And so she went in.

Will you go in for this peace—this deeper richer peace, this second rest, this peace of God to garrison your heart and mind?

5

The Christian's Power

This time I am going to speak about the POWER of the Christian life, and my text is in Acts i., 8 :—

" Ye shall receive power after that the Holy Ghost is come upon you."

Half-starved Christians say, " We got everything when we got converted, and now we are looking for the Lord's coming." But this chapter does not agree with that.

We read (ii., 4) that " they were all filled with the Holy Ghost and began to speak with other tongues "—not *unknown tongues,* but *other* tongues. What kind of tongues? It is said " Every man heard them speak in his own language, and they were all amazed, saying, are not all these that speak Galileans? how do we hear every man in our own language? " The miracle was not in the *tongues,* but in the *ears.* " How hear we every man? " Peter is talking as a Galilean, and yet there are seven different tongues heard. Supposing I was speaking as they did on the day of Pentecost, and was speaking English, there would be a German hearing German, a Frenchman hearing French, and so on. There was only one man talking, and, whatever happened between Peter's tongue and the other's ears, the miracle was there. When they tell you that the gift of tongues is the sign and seal of the baptism of the Holy Spirit, there is not a single word in the Bible for it.

"Ye shall receive power." The heart of man desires power more than anything else. We see it in children. It is intensified in young men and women. I do not know whether you are in middle life or older, there is in every one of us the instinct that desires power. Some men desire money that they may have power. They do not give two straws for the money, it is only for what money can give them. They wish to dominate the finance of the country and the markets of the country. The politician tells you before the election what he is going to do. What he wants is the opportunity to wield power and influence. Or a man gives himself to study in order to get power. Everywhere, among all classes and conditions, there is this universal desire for power.

We boast about our religion that it is a religion of power. We glory in the Cross of Christ "towering o'er the wrecks of time." It is the marvellous power in Christ and in this Gospel that is our boast. We cannot boast of that too much; but there is a difference between what you read to-day in the Bible and its manifestation in your life. The world is concerned more about the power in your life than about what you say. They have a right to know and see the expression of that power in your life and mine. The Lord told His disciples "Ye shall receive power." Are you living the powerless or paralysed life? Is your life full of energy Divine? or is it a life where the paramount thing is weakness? Here is what the Word of God says, and here is how I live: Do they correspond? Is my life a life of power or of paralysis? Am I being wheeled around like a paralytic invalid? or am I a mighty man helping on the work of Christ in the strength of God? Is the life full of Divine energy or of human weakness? is it a life of failure or of victory? Are you triumphing in Christ, or are the devil and the world triumphing over you?

If you are not able to answer that question there are three who know, (1) The *devil* knows: He is a keen discerner of things. He has a great interest in you since you got converted. Next to God, nobody studies us like the devil. He sees every move. He knows whether you are living a powerful or a paralysed life. We may be ministers, evangelists, pilgrim preachers, Sunday School teachers, or speakers in the open air; but we do not bluff the devil. He knows exactly our weight and measure.

When I was in charge of a church in Glasgow one of the converts made a request that caused a laugh. He prayed "Lord give me a good reputation in hell with the devil." Afterwards I said to him, "Johnny, I want to see you. Now, listen! I do not want to put a curb on you, but I would not say a thing to make us laugh at the Prayer Meeting." He said, "I did not say it to make you laugh. I was praying the desire of my heart; I got it in God's Word." I said, "Where?" He replied, "Do you remember where the devil said 'Jesus we know, and Paul we know, but who are you?' I would not like the devil to have to say to me 'Who are you?' I do pray that God will give me a good reputation with the devil." (2) The *world* knows it too. We can preach the most eloquent sermon, and go through all the stunts, but they have got the thing sized up. I mean the world you mingle with in your business and social engagements; they have got your size and measure, and know just exactly what kind of life you are living. If you and I don't know, they know it.

(3) The *Lord Jesus* knows every one of us. He has our weight, size, and measure. How he longs that this fulness of His should be mine! There may be a possible D. L. Moody reading this who will be used of God to turn the world upside down. Who knows of the latent undeveloped possibilities there are in a life? What a mighty channel of blessing God might make of your life!

John, in his Gospel, gives us three portraits of a powerless man. The first is the one who came to Jesus by night. He was principal of the Theological College in Jerusalem. We never knew a theological man to do much for God. God takes the nobodies to confound the somebodies: "not many wise are called." If we wanted somebody to do something, *we* would get somebody with the initials of the alphabet after his name; but God takes up Billy so-and-so. Nicodemus was a religious sneak, and shrank from the open. If you had said, in a meeting where he was, "Everybody who is saved, will you kindly rise," he would have said, "I do not believe in that, I do not like these emotional meetings."

The second is the case of Lazarus who was raised from the dead. He had all his grave-clothes on and had to be loosed. A live man tied up in his grave clothes with a napkin about his mouth! Do you know any Lazaruses? They are saved, no doubt, but they have no liberty. They are tied hand and foot by the tyranny of public opinion. They are bound and gripped by fetters far stronger than ever gripped any slave in the Southern States of America. All they can do is to walk to church.

The third portrait is that of a big blustering sailor like myself. I will rub shoulders with Peter when I get to heaven. I do love poor impulsive Peter. "Though all forsake You, Lord, it is not me! I'm the boy who will stand by You." The Lord said, "You will deny Me." "Deny You, Jesus? You made a mistake! I am going to die for You." A waiting-maid comes along next morning, and he falls. Peter was not the first man who fell before a woman. You remember the case of Elijah and Jezebel. When Jezebel sent him a love-letter he took to his heels and ran. A girl comes along to Peter, and the next thing is that he is cursing and denying his Lord. He was a big strong man, but just a bag of wind when you struck him. How many Peters are there? "Lord, I will show them how to be a Christian." I know some like that in my own town and they are dumb to-day. Somebody put a pin in them, and their wind came out—nothing better than penny balloons! Somebody slanders them, or did them an ill-turn. The church looked kind of dead, and all the wind is out of them.

What word portraits John gives us of these men. Poor Nicodemus, with all his scholarship, refinement, and culture, just a timid, shy, trembling kind of sneak! Lazarus, with all the life he had, tied hand and foot! Peter, with all the blustering impulse, denying and cursing before the sneer of a maid.

You need not be like that any longer. This man Peter received power after that the Holy Ghost came upon him, and he walked right through with steadfastness of aim, bringing the very blood of Christ upon His murderers, and then walking to die as his Lord died—but with his head down—on a cross. In spite of your past failure and weakness, and of the bankruptcy of your past experience, and of the slavery and bondage you have endured, and of that creeping paralysis, it may be all changed. "Ye shall receive power." The weakest man can be stronger than hell. The weakest and most timid shy woman may become a lion for God. It will not make you tremble any less, but it will put passion and energy into you that will overcome every obstacle.

When Lord Roberts' son was at Spion Kop, he was accompanied by a lot of fine brave young Britishers who seemed careless of danger. They rushed in a battery and it was to certain death. Young Roberts was noticed by one of them to be pale, and was accused of cowardliness; to which the reply was made, "If you were half as scared as I feel, you would take to your heels and run."

There is a courage which can stand firm in spite of all natural timorousness. God can enable us to say, "When I am weak, then am I strong." However paralysed your experience may have been, that may be at an end. "Ye shall receive power." But—"tarry." How long?—"Until." I cannot tell you how long. Tarry *until* something happens.

Some tarry a long time. The apostles tarried ten days. After two or three days Peter may have got up and said, "I feel I must make a confession, I denied Jesus and cursed and swore." He sits down, and then I can see Thomas getting up and saying, "Well, if Peter confessed, I need to make a confession too. I said that, unless I put my fingers into His wounds, I would not believe. I cannot tell you how sorry I feel." I can see John Mark getting up and saying, " Well, if Peter and Thomas had a confession, I have one too, I took to my heels and ran, I forsook him." (Mark xiv., 51, 52). Another would say, " I would not believe that He rose from the dead."

That was a great ten days. They tarried until, *until;* and, glory to God, when the tarrying was done the Holy Ghost fell on them. The reason why so few Acts of the Apostles are being written is because so few of those that came to Calvary have gone on to the upper room, to be purified and baptised with the Holy Ghost. Tarry until everything is on the altar, every wrong righted, every confession made. There is no waiting on God's part; He is readier to bless than we are to be blessed; but tarry *until*—whether it is all night, all day, or six months. I used to look at Christians and say, " Well, you want this blessing; well now, just take it by faith, it is all right." All they got was credulity.

A minister came to me and said, " All I have for my faith to rest upon for my salvation is a piece of paper. I was anxious about my soul, and they told me 'Do you see that—John iii., 16?' 'Yes.' 'Do you believe it?' 'Yes.' 'Well, you are saved.' " Thank God for a piece of paper with the Word of God on it. Thank God for the blue piece of paper, my marriage lines, but I have got the woman herself. Thank God for the Holy Ghost, I have got Him Himself. I tarried *until*—.There were a lot of things to be made right, a whole lot of wrongs to be righted. There was the question of my Presbyterian reputation. I tarried in the town of Bangor *until;* and then everything was ready. I could tell you the very place where it happened, round the Pickie—not one moment too soon, and not one moment too late.

Do you know this power? Are you in the enjoyment and under the sway and domination of it? Is there a hunger in your heart for it?

All the promises are yea and amen. I like the meaning of that phrase. It is like this: "God, I am in Christ." "Yes." "Here is the promise—you shall receive power when the Holy Ghost is come upon you. Is that for me or for the Jew?" "Yea, it is for you," and then I say, "Amen, it shall be mine." Will you do that now? You say "I know Jesus as my Saviour: are all the promises, then, yea and amen?" "Yes." "All right, God." "Ye shall receive power." "When?" "After the Holy Ghost is come upon you."

He never gives you any power apart from His government. It is not *my* using *Him*, but *His* using *me*. When did you receive pardon? After ye believed. When do you receive power? After the Holy Ghost is come upon you. When does He come? Tarry until. Do not take any credulity, and *imagine* you have got it when you have not. You know when everything is on the altar, and when there is a willingness to go through with Christ, and take up the Cross, saying, "Jesus, I am going through," glory to God, you know. Then, instead of failure and paralysis, there will be power, joy, victory, peace, and wonderful fruitfulness in God's service.

"Thy Holy Spirit, Lord, alone can turn our hearts from sin:
His power alone can sanctify, and make us pure within.
O Spirit of faith and love, come in our midst, we pray,
And purify each waiting heart! Baptise us with power to-day."

6
The Fulness of the Spirit

MANY people are deceived and think they are *exempt* from conversion, because they have, as they say, "always loved the Lord." "They were baptised into covenant grace," and then "they joined the Church." and since then "have lived a fairly respectable, religious life," attending their church regularly and supporting it generously, so they are quite satisfied they are exempt from conversion. They believe others may require it, but they don't. They do not deny the *fact* of conversion. Oh, no; they just think it is not for them. In fact they are highly insulted and feel indignant if any one dares to question them about their being converted. The sad thing too, is that very little, if anything, is ever said about the *necessity* and *nature* of it by their minister. Believe me, dear friend, without conversion you will never enter the kingdom of heaven. The only kind of people there are converted people. Hear the words of the Lord Jesus, "Verily I say unto you, except ye be converted and become as little children, *ye shall not* enter the kingdom of heaven." So we see the absolute necessity for being converted, if we are ever to enter the kingdom of heaven. If you could enter heaven without conversion, you would succeed in making Jesus Christ a LIAR. Remember this one thing—*You don't need to be converted if you have made up your mind to go to hell.* There are no converted people there.

SELF-DECEIVED

On the other hand, there are many who say "they have been converted," and merely deceive themselves, because they give no evidence in their lives of being converted. If their lives do not bear the fruit of conversion, what right have they to profess conversion? They are merely dupes of the devil, deceiving themselves and damning their own souls. Jesus has said, "By their

FRUITS (not by their *profession*) ye shall know them." The last logical argument to any man regarding the nature of a tree is the fruit it bears. So it is in the converted life. No matter what profession we make, or have made, if our lives are not a confirmation of the fact, we are only religious HUM-BUGS or hypocrites, for "Not everyone that saith unto Me Lord, Lord, shall enter the kingdom of heaven, but he that DO-ETH (keeps on doing) the will of my Father." So let us examine ourselves *carefully* and *scripturally*, and see whether we are converted or not. Let me ask you, dear reader, some plain questions which will help you to see whether you are converted or not.

I.—Are you fully surrendered to the Lord Jesus.

Do you daily desire to know, and endeavour to do His will? You may do everything but this, but there is no true conversion until this takes place. Many will pray and agonize and give up anything and everything, or attempt to work for Christ and the Church, but all these are no substitutes for surrender of the will to Christ. When Saul or Tarsus was converted that day on the road to Damascus, he cried, "What wilt thou have me to do?" And you are not truly converted until you have come to the same place of surrender to the will of Christ. The Lord never saves us to do what we like or live as we like. We are converted that we might serve Him in "righteousness and true holiness all the days of our life without fear." Another question:—

II.—Has the burden of sin been removed, and have you now peace WITH God? If so, you FEEL and know there is therefore NOW no condemnation. The sense of guilt and fear has all gone. "The Spirt answers to the Blood and tells me I am born of God." The peace of God fills your mind and heart. The *consciousness* of this experience may have come slowly or suddenly. But slow or sudden, every truly converted person experiences this removal of the burden of guilt and condemnation. There is no true conversion apart from this. Again:—

III.—Has there come into your heart a new feeling of love to Christ and Christians! Has the enmity been slain? Has the fear and dread been removed, and can you now sing "My Jesus I love Thee, I KNOW Thou art mine." Instead of His presence giving you *pain*, it now thrills you with *pleasure*, and you also want to make the Christians your companions, for you desire fellowship with them. You used to shun them and miscall them, but now they are your "choice" friends. You have real love for them. This is not *natural*. It is natural to hate the Lord's people and the Lord, for the natural mind is enmity against the Lord. This new love is a *supernatural* love, and a sure evidence that you are truly converted. Again:—

IV.—Have you a relish and desire for God's Word? You maybe used to read it sometimes, but it was so uninteresting and mysterious. Now, however, you are surprised how interesting it is and how easily understood. You read it now with real relish, and delight to go where it is expounded and explained.

V.—Has secret prayer not only become a necessity but a real luxury? You don't merely do it because you feel it is your duty, but you delight in it. It is no longer a sort of *penance*, but a *privilege* and *pleasure*. You know now what is meant by "stealing away to Jesus." "Fellowship with Jesus, oh, what blessed sweet communion." Also:—

VI.—Does pain come to your heart now because of sin and sinful thoughts? There was a day when you revelled and rioted in sin. Sin was a painful thing only when you were found out in it, but now you feel real pain and grief and long for full deliverance from it. Your constant prayer and desire is for the Lord to make you as sinless as a saved sinner can be made on the road to heaven. Even the *appearance* of sin is now painful; and as for sinful thoughts, they are abhorred by you and not secretly indulged in any longer. Your conscience and Christ are close companions. If not, there can be no true conversion.

VII.—Do you experience deep humility and self-abasement daily? Once you were proud and boasted about your good deeds and self-righteousness. Now you abhor yourself, and like Job, repent in dust and ashes. Your constant cry is:—

"Oh, to be saved from myself, dear Lord;
Oh, to be lost in Thee;
Oh, that it might be no more 'I'
But Christ who lives in me."

Your wonder now is that Christ should ever have loved and saved such a sinner. Like the old Puritan, you say, "I have no quarrel with what Paul said when he said he was 'the CHIEF of sinners,' but I do quarrel with him for taking my place." You feel your righteousnesses are now as FILTHY rags and your good works mere refuse.

VIII.—Have you a growing desire after holiness and likeness to Christ? There is nothing so beautiful to you now as the "beauty of holiness." Like the Psalmist you cry, "As the hart pants after water-brooks, so pants my soul after Thee." Oh, how you pant for likeness to Him and holiness, without which no man shall see the Lord. Therefore you are perfecting holiness in the fear of the Lord daily.

IX.—Is there a real desire and an honest effort to save the lost? Does the "thud of Christless feet on the road to hell" sound in your ears daily, and are you moved with compassion for the perishing? Can you in some measure say and feel with the poet as he wrote about Paul—

"Oft when the word is on me to deliver,
Lifts the illusion and the truth lies bare;
Desert or throng, the city or the river,
Melts in a lucid paradise of air:
Only like souls I see the folk thereunder
Bound, who should conquer; slaves, who should be kings;
Hearing their one hope with an empty wonder,
Sadly contented with the show of things—
Then with a rush, *the intolerable craving*
Shivers through me like a trumpet call—
Oh, to save them; to perish for their saving,
Die for their life—be offered for them all."

These are a few evidences that always result from a genuine conversion. They may not all be as evident to yourself or to others, or as fully evident as you or they would desire. But in some measure and in some degree they are there. There is first the blade and then the ear and then the full corn in the ear. You can humbly and truly claim to be converted as you honestly examine yourself in the light of these evidences.

IF NOT, WHY NOT?

But if, dear reader, after reading these evidences, you begin to wonder whether you are truly converted or not, wouldn't it be wise to make sure about it, *and right now?* Don't be annoyed and feel angry at what you have read, but thank God that He led you to read these clear evidences, and thank God for the one who gave you the booklet to read. Your eyes are now open to see you are only a PROFESSOR of conversion and not a POSSESSOR of it. Turn to the Lord Jesus Christ just now, as you are, without one plea, and turning away from all sin and sinful ways, and self-righteous rags, and good works, and your fears and doubts, accept Him now as your personal Saviour and Lord and Master. He will receive you and save you, for "him that cometh to Me I will in no wise cast out," but "by Me if any man enter in he shall be saved and go in and out and find pasture"; and "no man can pluck them out of My hand," for "He is able to keep you from falling and to present you faultless before the presence of His glory with exceeding joy." "Only trust Him, only trust Him NOW."

THEN WHAT?

Now that you are converted, and SURE you are converted, THEN WHAT? I believe there are many truly converted, and they have made no further progress because of defeat and failure in their lives. They don't know there is anything after conversion but "doing the best they can," and as a consequence they know more about *defeat* than *victory*. More about *sighing* than *singing*. *Devoted* to their Lord, but daily *defeated* by the world, the flesh and the devil. Living a sort of treadmill existence, or a sort of *rolly-coaster* or *switchback* experience, up and down—but mostly down. Round and round they go day after day, getting nowhere, but coming right back to where they started. All motion but no progress. Like sitting in a rocking chair, swinging backward and forward, but always about in the same place. Five, ten, twenty years after their conversion and you find them just about where they started —if anything, they have backslidden. Poor souls. They are a disgust to themselves and a disgrace to the Lord and the Church. They can sing the words of the hymn:—

> "Once I thought I walked with Jesus,
> Ah, what changeful moods I had—
> Sometimes trusting, sometimes doubting,
> Sometimes joyful, sometimes sad."

LIVING ABNORMALLY

This is the AB-normal, God-dishonouring, Christ-disgracing, heart-disgusting sort of life many converted people live, all because they do not know that there is something *AFTER* conversion for them, and all IN Christ Jesus. The worst of it is, many have been led to think that this sort of life is the NORMAL life, and you can never expect any better until you get to heaven. They speak as if the AB-normal life was the life of victory and holiness and soul-winning. Why, it is just the reverse. Thank God there is a place IN Christ where every converted soul can be completely satisfied in Him, and experience Christ celebrating His victory in their lives before their enemies daily. But this is not the *crown* of honest effort or the *reward* for diligent and faithful service. No, emphatically NO; for it is "not of works lest any should boast." It is "*not* by might or by power, but by My Spirit saith the Lord." We often sing—would God we believed it and put it into practice—

> "Every virtue we possess and every victory won,
> Every thought of holiness are His and His ALONE."

HAVE YE RECEIVED?

So, after answering the question, "Am I converted?" there is another question—"Have ye received the Holy Ghost SINCE ye believed?" This was Paul's question to the Ephesian converts of Apollos. You remember Christ told His converted followers to "Tarry UNTIL ye be endued with power from on high." They were to "WAIT for *the* promise of the Father." What is this "enduement of power from on high?" This "*The* promise of the Father?" We are not left in any doubt about it, for the Lord Jesus told us "John baptised with water, but ye shall be baptised with the Holy Ghost not many days hence," and ten days after that they "were all *filled* with the Holy Ghost." To be *filled* with the Holy Ghost is to be baptised with the Holy Ghost. Let me ask you, dear reader—Have you received this baptism? Are you a Spirit-baptised and fire-swept believer?

NOT THE SAME AS CONVERSION

Let us remember that this blessing is not the same as conversion or being born again, and does not take place at the same time. It is always a *deeper* and a *second experience.* I suppose there is no reason why we should not be converted and baptised and filled with the Holy Spirit at the same time, but this never takes place to-day, and the Word of God teaches it always as a *second*, separable blessing from conversion. The disciples lived for three years, enjoying the greatest training and teaching men could enjoy. Christ was their Teacher. Just imagine living daily under Christ's personal supervision and influence and teaching, and that for three years. Surely they were fully equipped for life and service? Oh, no, for to these very men Jesus said, "*Tarry* until ye be endued with power from on high." "*Wait* for the promise of the Father." "Ye shall receive power *after* the Holy Ghost is come upon you, and ye shall be witnesses unto Me." So they "*tarried*," they "waited" until the "Day of Pentecost *fully came*," and they "were all *filled* with the Holy Spirit," and then began their wonderful ministry and martyrdom. If they required this enduement after three years of teaching and training by Jesus, if they were ever to live victorious, holy lives, and labour successfully in winning men for Christ, do we not need to obey the very same command, "tarry"—"wait"—until we are endued with power from on high? Who would dare to deny our need of a personal Pentecost to-day, in the face of so much failure and defeat in converted lives and so much barrenness in service for God?

PRE-PENTECOSTAL BELIEVERS

So many converted people are living BEFORE Pentecost in their experience instead of AFTER Pentecost. They know Christ as their personal Saviour, but not as the "*Baptiser*" with the Holy Ghost and fire. They have been to Calvary for the cleansing blood but they have never gone to Jerusalem for the Pentecost which would enable them to live lives of holiness, boldness and power. As a consequence they have a feeling of disappointment regarding Christ and His salvation. They expected victory and power when they came to Him for salvation, but instead of that it has just been the reverse. They haven't heard about the Baptism with the Holy Ghost and fire, that it is their birthright blessing. You remember the Ephesian converts were just the same. Paul asked them, "Have ye received the Holy Ghost SINCE ye believed?" They said, "We have not so much as heard whether there be any Holy Ghost." So many are just in the same plight to-day. No wonder their lives are so unsatisfying and unsatisfactory to Christ and to themselves.

DEFINITE AND CONSCIOUS

Let us remember also that this blessing is a very *definite* and *conscious* experience. Just as definite as conversion and just as conscious an experience as conversion. There was a moment when you were not converted. Then you decided for Christ, and that moment you were converted. It is just as definite as marriage. One moment you are not married, but when you say "I will," that very moment you are married. A very definite and real experience. It is just as definite as Church membership. There was a time when you were not a member, but you became a candidate for membership and were accepted, and in a moment's time you become a member. A very definite and very real experience. So it is, dear reader, with the baptism with the Holy Spirit. You are converted when you repent of your sins and believe on the Lord Jesus Christ, and *suddenly* converted too. You are baptised and filled with the Holy Spirit when you *surrender* fully and *receive* by faith the Holy Spirit. This is no hazy or ambiguous, indefinite, gradual experience. It is a *sudden*, conscious, blessed experience. You know when it takes place, and so does everybody else you come in contact with. Yet there are so many who pray and desire this blessing, but never definitely experience it. But worse still, Satan gets them to stay right there in that condition, content with merely a pious wish or desire, but no experience. Every time they hear a message about this blessing and receive an invitation to accept it, they go through the same routine again, and put up their hand, they come forward to the altar, and pray and wait, but never get any farther. The time comes when they either *despair* of the blessing or they *despise* it.

Dear reader, don't let Satan deprive you of this all-essential blessing by making you satisfied with merely asking and waiting, but never receiving.

A REVOLUTIONARY EXPERIENCE

Another thing to remember about the Baptism with the Holy Spirit is this—*It is a revolutionary experience* in the life. There are many quiet amiable people who have been brought up in Godly homes, and the Sunday School and Church, and lived religious lives. When they get converted there is not a very great change in their life *outwardly*. They continue going to their Church and saying their prayers and reading their Bible, and living a decent, respectable sort of Christian life. You would hardly know they have been converted, but when they have been baptised with the Holy Spirit, what a revolutionary change takes place. The disciples *before* and *after* Pentecost are an example of this. They are now on fire for the Lord and the souls of men and women. They not merely love the Lord, they are IN LOVE with the Lord. That's a tremendous difference. They live on the *singing* side of Salvation now, because they are victorious and successful. Christ is not merely a ROOT out of a dry ground to their souls. He is the Rose of Sharon, the Lily of the Valley, the fairest among ten thousand to their souls. They do not *endure* salvation—they *enjoy* it. You see it is the Holy Spirit's work to make Christ *real*, and make all He purchased for us with His blood a reality in heart and life daily. So when we receive Him, He glorifies Christ IN us and TO us, and Christ becomes a very satisfying reality to the Pentecostal believer. Without this blessing your life will never be pleasing to God or a blessing to your fellow-men, in the fulness God intended it to be, and Christ died to make possible. But it will be always *disobedient*, *inconsistent*, and *incomplete*.

NOT CERTAIN

I can imagine you saying to me, "I am not sure whether this blessing is mine or not. God knows I have desired it, and have even gone the length of going forward to the altar as an indication that I had decided to have it, but I can never say I have been baptised and filled with the Holy Spirit." Let me try and show you how you may know whether you have received the blessing or not.

HOW YOU MAY KNOW

If you have NOT received this blessing there will be:—

I.—A Sense of Orphanage instead of Sonship. There are times when you are not sure whether you are born again or not. You feel like an orphan. You cannot say for *sure* that God is your Father. Sometimes you *believe* you are a child of God, and sometimes you wonder whether you are or not. If you are asked, "Are you truly converted?" you answer "I *hope* I am," or "I *think* I am." Or perhaps you say, "I *trust* I am," or "I *believe* I am," but you are never willing, nor are you able to say "I am *sure* I am"—"I *know* I am." This is because you have not been baptised and filled with the Holy Spirit. For one of the first things He does when He comes is to *testify* of Jesus, and He does it in such a way that you never again have a doubt about your relationship to God. You FEEL and KNOW from that time you are a Son of God and joint-heir with Jesus Christ.

Again you may know you have not been baptised and filled with the Holy Spirit, because:—

II.—There is a deadness to the things of God instead of to the world. You have more interest and pleasure in reading a novel than reading the Bible. You like to listen to men, but never feel inclined to take the time and the bother to listen to God, by His Spirit, through His Word. A prayer meeting has little or no attraction for you, but a picture show or some social function charms and thrills you. The preaching of the Word puts you to sleep, but a lecture on politics, travel, art or science, intensely interests you. Sunday and the House of God have no attraction for you. If it is wet or cold or too hot, you desecrate the one and forsake the other, by absenting yourself. But Monday morning sees you vigorous and well and early making for your place of business. Even to THINK of a whole night in prayer would shock and weary you, but to spend hours in some home at a social function or in the lodge or club is a joy and pleasure. To engage in a conversation with another Christian about heavenly things is well nigh impossible, for you are densely ignorant about them, but to talk about sport or politics or business or social gossip, you can wax eloquent. To give generously and regularly to the work of God in your Church, is quite a hardship, and makes you feel like a martyr or a philanthropist, but to support your club or lodge or political party is such a pleasure. If there is any retrenching to be done, along the line of giving, you never think of cutting out the lodge or club dues, but you start right in with the little you give to the Lord and His Church. You spend dollars on holidays and cents on Christ's cause. You may be sure you have never been baptised and filled with the Holy Spirit where such a condition as this exists.

You may know that you have not been baptised and filled with the Holy Spirit because:—

III.—You are in Bondage instead of Liberty. Oh, how many sons of God there are who are slaves to the world, the flesh and the devil. You have been redeemed by Blood and Power, but you are still in bondage and misery. You are in bondage to the fear of man, to public opinion, to the customs and conventionalities of society. To become "*unusual*" or "*peculiar*" for the Lord fills you with abject terror. To be noted for good works, and zealous for piety and holiness, is something to shun and dread, and far from being desired, because the carnal Christians and ungodly people might deride you. What pure delight and real joy such a person must give to the devil, what grief and keen pain he must give to the Lord Jesus.

Another very sure evidence that you have not been baptised and filled with the Holy Spirit is this:—

IV.—Barrenness instead of Fruitfulness in life and service.

You have never, or rarely ever, had the joy of winning a soul to the Lord. You may have preached for years, or taught Sunday School, or trained your children in the home, but never a soul won for the Lord. Your life yields no fruit unto holiness. The fruit of the Spirit—love, joy, peace, etc.—is stunted and warped. No one knows all this better than yourself, and many a time you have had strange stirrings of discontent and dissatisfaction on account of it, and longings to be fruitful in every good work, increasing in the knowledge of the Lord. Thank God, such a life of orphanage, deadness, bondage and barrenness can end, and end SUDDENLY. The moment you receive the Holy Spirit it is His office and work to do this and far more for you. It is all yours already IN Christ Jesus, and the Holy Spirit will take of the things of Christ and make them yours in reality and experience. Sorrowing and sighing will cease and songs and everlasting joy will crown your life.

NOT TO PRAY FOR THE HOLY SPIRIT

There are many people to-day, some of them well-known men, and excellent men, too, who tell us that we ought not to pray for the Holy Spirit, and they reason it out very speciously. They say, "The Holy Spirit was given to the Church as an abiding possession" (and that is true), and then they ask, "Why pray for what you have already got?" To this the late Dr. A. J. Gordon replied conclusively, "Jesus Christ was given to the world as *an abiding gift* at Calvary. He was given to the world as a whole, but each individual in the world must appropriate this gift for himself. Just so the gift of the Holy Spirit was given to the Church as a whole, but each individual member of the Church must appropriate this gift for himself, and God's way of appropriation is PRAYER."

WE HAVE THE HOLY SPIRIT

Here is something we need to remember—that every born again one HAS the Holy Spirit, for "if we have not the Spirit of Christ we are none of His." But the difference is this, it is one thing for us to have the Holy Spirit, but it is altogether a different matter for Him to have full possession of us. Every born again one is not baptised and filled with the Holy Spirit, and never can or will be until He is received by them. When you are born again, that brings you eternal life, but when you are baptised and filled with the Holy Spirit that brings you not only life, but LIFE MORE ABUNDANT.

TARRYING

Let me say a word about "Tarrying"—"Waiting," that we hear so much about these days. Remember that the "Tarrying" the "Waiting" is not on God's side, it is on ours. He says, "*If* ye being evil know how to give good gifts to your children HOW MUCH MORE shall your heavenly Father give you the Holy Spirit." The "Waiting" the "Tarrying" is on our side, for it takes us such a long time to get all on the altar—we are so slow and stubborn. There are things we know that we must yield, and things that must be put right, and before our wills are bent and willing to do it, it is generally a long time. This is where the "Tarrying" comes in, but the very moment our all is on the altar and every controversy settled, between us and the Lord, the Holy Spirit takes possession of us and we *know* it has happened. For the Spirit is given to those who OBEY as well as those who BELIEVE. It takes time to get to the place where "WE LET GO, and LET GOD." But we are to "Tarry"—How long? UNTIL—until when? Until we are endued with power from on high. God demands and will have nothing *less* or *else* than an ABSOLUTE SURRENDER. He does not demand a *perfect* surrender—if He did, we could never give it—but He does demand an *honest* surrender. There must be no reservations or evasions in heart, mind, or life. "We can never prove the delights of His love *until* ALL on the altar we lay."

THOSE WHO THIRST

Having read thus far you must surely have been brought to see and believe that there is such a blessing as the baptism and fulness of the Holy Spirit, for every truly converted one. You believe it is a definite, revolutionary, real, experience, always received AFTER conversion, never AT conversion. You have been brought to *know* and *feel* your need of it, not only through reading this, but also by your painful past experience of dissatisfaction, defeat and failure. You know now, as never before, from reading God's Word, and seeing the lives of others, who have received this blessing, that such a life of defeat and failure is a dishonour to God and His Church. All this has filled you with an intense desire, a "thirst" for this blessing. Thank God for this, for Jesus has said, "If any man thirst . . . this spake He of the Spirit which they that believe *should* receive."

WARNING

Let me sound out a note of warning right here. There are those who sneer, and despise, and ridicule this teaching, and ignore the blessing, and do despite to the Holy Spirit thereby. Yet Jesus said, "It is expedient for you that I go away, for if I go not away the Comforter will not come to you." That is, it is more necessary for Me to go and for Him to come to you, than for Me to stay and Him not to come. Yet they say we are slighting the Lord Jesus when we honour the Spirit. I believe such an attitude is of the devil, and encouraged by him to keep us out of our Pentecostal blessing. Be warned, dear friend, whatever your reasons may be for despising and rejecting the baptism and fulness of the Holy Spirit, the Lord may swear in His wrath that ye shall not enter into His rest. The children of Israel despised the promised land, by refusing to enter into it, and the Lord deprived them of the possibility of entering in. Esau despised his birthright by selling it for a mess of pottage and when with tears he would have sought and found it he wasn't able. Let these incidents be a warning to you not to despise and sell out your Pentecostal birthright blessing or the time may come when you will see what you have lost, but find it out too late, and your life remain barren, and parched, and then, when standing before the Judgement Seat of Christ, you will find your life nothing but "faded leaves instead of ripened fruit." A soul saved, but *a life lost*, and lost for ever. *Saved so as by fire*. Saved by the skin of your teeth.

Let me point out to you who are seeking this most blessed and necessary experience (not necessary to salvation, but absolutely necessary for a holy victorious, soul-winning life), there are at least three steps necessary—simple steps, that all may take who are willing,

STEPS INTO THIS BLESSING

I.—Cleansing. It is one thing to be forgiven, but it is quite another thing to be *cleansed.* You may be *pardoned* and yet not *purified.* You may have the new heart, that is, regenerated, and yet not have the *clean heart.* David received forgiveness from the Lord for His foul sin. Nathan said to him, "The Lord also hath put away thy sin," but that was not enough for David, he cried out for cleansing in the 51st Psalm, "Create in me a *clean* heart." This is something over and above and beyond, and deeper than forgiveness. In 1st John 1. 7, we read, "The blood of Jesus Christ His Son *cleanseth* us from all sin," and in 1st John 1. 9, "He is faithful and just to forgive us our sins and to *cleanse* us from all unrighteousness." Is the cleansing of verse 7 the same as the cleansing of verse 9? Most certainly not. The cleansing of verse 7 has to do with the GUILT of sin—with sin *after* it has been committed; this is the only sense in which the blood of Jesus cleanses—it washes white as snow from the guilt and stain of actual transgression—that cleansing is *retrospective.* Now this cleansing of verse 7 is the forgiving of verse 9; both these words bear a sinner's justification. But the "*cleansing* from all unrighteousness" of verse 9 is something different from, something over and above the "forgiving" of verse 9 or the "cleansing" of verse 7; else, if they mean one and the same thing, would not the author be guilty of tautology? The "cleansing" of verse 9 is prospective, and refers to holiness of life—to our being saved from sin and sinning.

Before we can ever be cleansed from all unrighteousness, there must be humble and honest *confession*—definite, honest confession. No hiding of sin in any way, shape or form. No covering it up or making any excuse or apology for it. Confession implies renunciation—a willingness to be done with it for ever. It is pure mockery to confess our sin and expect to continue in it afterwards. We must turn from it with full purpose of heart and honestly confess it. Name it, whatever the thing may be. Be drastic and definite about it. As surely as we do, we are forgiven and cleansed. You need not ask the Lord to forgive you or cleanse you, for He "*IS*"—not *was*, or *will be*, but "*IS*" faithful and just to forgive and cleanse. The moment we confess our sin—that moment—we are forgiven and cleansed, whether we FEEL it or not. God IS faithful and just, no matter how or what we feel about the matter. Until you believe this you will never get any farther.

II.—Absolute surrender. This is the second step we must take if we are to be baptised and filled with the Holy Spirit. We must surrender ALL, without any *reservation* or *evasion* in mind or in life. The blood that *cleanses* now *claims* us, and ALL of us. It must be "I'll be what you want me to be"; "I'll go where you want me to go"; "I'll do what you want me to do." The reason so many never enter into a definite experience is right here. They try to play the same game on the Lord that Ananias and Sapphira did with the apostles—"Holding back part of the price." We may deceive others, and even succeed in deceiving ourselves, but we can never deceive the Lord Jesus, and it is with Him we are dealing. He knows when our "all" is on the altar, and will "tarry" until our "all" is on the altar. He will take nothing *else* or *less* than our "all." ALL includes everything and excludes nothing. He knows when our all is fully yielded, and until it is will never baptise and fill us with His Holy Spirit. "No withholding, full confession, riches, pleasures, ALL must flee." It is strange how fear begins to fill the mind and heart when we are at the altar of consecration. You would think, the way some halt and hesitate, that Christ was some brutal and tyrannical monster. Reader, don't you know that the Lord Jesus is the LOVER of your soul? There is no one who loves you so warmly or so well as He does. There is no one who desires your best interests, temporal and eternal, as He does. No good thing will He withhold from you. He has your best interests at heart. *You couldn't begin to love yourself as He loves you.* It is perfectly safe to surrender your all fully to Him.

WHY FEARFUL?

I wonder whether the fear that arises when we come to the time and place of absolute surrender is not caused by something wrong in the past, and something that has to be made right. As you "tarry" it rises up out of the past and comes before your mind. Some one you wronged long ago. Some debt contracted and forgotten. Something stolen from another, not much maybe, only a mere trifle, yet stolen. Hear what the Lord says about it: "Therefore, if thou bring thy gift to the altar and THERE *remember* . . . leave there thy gift before the altar, and go thy way, first be reconciled to thy brother, and THEN *come* and offer thy gift." There must be restitution if some wrong in the past has been done. It must be put right. There must be reconciliation. Grudge and bitterness must be confessed, and forgiveness granted by the party you held the grudge or bitterness against. I believe it is here so many fail to receive the baptism and fulness of the Spirit. They are unwilling to make the surrender complete. The Lord does not bring these things up out of our past to tease or torment us. No, He desires us to be right with our brother, so that we may win him for the Lord. Go THROUGH, dear reader, however humiliating and painful the process. It is the only way to fulness, victory and satisfaction.

WILLING TO BE MADE WILLING

Let me say here, that if you are dealing with the Lord about restitution or reconciliation, as you are now before the altar—that is surrendering. Tell Him you will right the wrong, as far as you can. You will seek the party as soon as you can and ask their forgiveness. You will acknowledge the debt and pay it just as soon as you can. If you do this, then, thank God, He will *take the will for the deed*, and lead you on into the blessing. But be very careful to be honest and sincere in this. The Lord will go farther. He will work in you and make you willing to do this, *if you are willing to be made willing*, and *enable* you to do it. He will "work in you to *will* and to do His good pleasure." Remember, He doesn't demand a *perfect* surrender, but He does demand an *honest* surrender—that is, all you know, and *all you don't know.* He will take nothing *else* or *less* than this.

III.—Receive by faith the baptism and fulness of the Holy Spirit. Jesus said to His disciples and He says to you, "Receive the Holy Ghost." There are so many and they fully surrender and make no other move, and then wonder why it is that they have not received the blessing. However willing a sinner may be to be saved, he isn't saved because he is *willing.* He is saved by *receiving* the Lord Jesus. We do not receive the enduement of power from on high until we receive the Holy Spirit. "Ye shall receive power *after* that the Holy Ghost is come upon you," but not until we *receive* Him. It is not credulity to do this. *It is faith in action.* Faith without works is dead. It isn't enough to be willing; you must venture by faith on the naked word of God. When you do this, and just as surely as you do it, then the Holy Spirit takes possession whether you feel it or not. God is true to His word no matter how you feel about it. He says: "Whatsoever things ye desire, when ye pray, believe that ye have them, *and ye shall have them.*" "This is the confidence that we have in Him, that if we ask anything according to His Will He heareth us; and if we know that He hear us, whatsoever we ask, we know we have the petitions that we desired of Him." You know it is God's will for you to be baptised and filled with the Holy Spirit. This was your petition you desired of Him, wasn't it? Then you know you *have* the petition—you have been baptised and filled with the Holy Spirit. God says it. So you can thankfully and humbly say you are now baptised and filled with the Holy Spirit.

FEELINGS

I can imagine you asking, "Will there never be any *feeling* about it? Will I never be *conscious* of the blessing? Will there be no *manifestation* of it?" Assuredly there will, but you must leave the *nature* of the manifestation to Him. You must leave the *time* when you receive the feeling or manifestation to Him. "But the manifestation is given to every man." It is not ours to be concerned about this; it is ours to be sure that we have truly and fully confessed and renounced all sin and absolutely surrendered our all to Him; and that as best we know how, we have received the Holy Spirit to fill us to the uttermost. God will take care of the feelings and the manifestation. He knows best just the time to give it to you, and the way to make you conscious of it.

TESTING

He may and generally does test our faith, by withholding any manifestation or feeling from us, but only for a time. When Jesus was baptised with the Holy Spirit at the Jordan, He was led by the Spirit into the wilderness to be tempted of the devil for forty days. While there He hungered, and there were wild beasts. But we read: "He came out of the wilderness full of the Holy Spirit," and so will you if you are willing to take Him at His word, and walk by *faith* and not feeling. You see, dear reader, signs never satisfied any sincere soul. They can be simulated, and they don't last. But the word of the Lord endures for ever. Better a million times one word from the Lord, than all the fanciest feelings and ecstatic experiences one could have, for "heaven and earth will pass away, but My word will never pass away." Hallelujah!

"I take the promised Holy Ghost,
I take the power of Pentecost,
To fill me now to the uttermost—
I take, He *undertakes*."

7
A Personal Testimony

"I lived in a distracted state for nearly seven months after my conversion. Some have told me I wasn't converted at all - that I only thought I was. But they were wrong. I was truly born again, and a new creature in Jesus Christ. I had the inward witness clear, and the outward evidence that I was a changed man . . . I hated sin, but was continually overcome by it. I loved holiness, and longed to be perfectly whole, but never experienced it. I was truly a child of God, but a slave of the devil. My life was up and down, but more down than up. I was committing sin and confessing it, but rarely having victory over it. I believed their was deliverance for me, but how to obtain it I didn't know.

"I knew some Christians who were living a victorious, joyous, soul-winning life. How I envied them! I am sure if I had only made known to them the fluctuating, failing kind of life I was living, they would have led me into the open secret; but I was ashamed to make my experience known . . .

"Thank God, the day of my deliverance was at hand. One of the leading businessmen of the town, an out-and-out man for Christ and souls, arranged for a 'Convention for the Deepening of the Christian Life.' My older brother, James, and a close friend of his in his student days, Reverend J. Stuart Holden, were the convention leaders.

"If they had called the conference 'holiness meetings' I would have been frightened, and would never have attended. I would have called them wild fire and fanaticism; and being a good, well behaved, blue-stockinged Presbyterian, I would have shunned them.

"From the very first sermon I heard, I was sure my brother had told Holden about me, for he made public my miserable condition. It made me feel clean mad! I determined I would not go to another service; but I was there the next night. I was more sure than ever that my brother had put the preacher up to preach at me. I became more angry every night, but could not keep myself from attendance.

"Stuart Holden made the secret of the victorious Christian life so clear and plain. After one has been born again by the Spirit of God he can live victoriously only by the Holy Spirit. I began to understand that I could not attain this life by self effort or ceremonies, for it was 'not by might nor by power, but by the Spirit.' It was not an *attainment,* but an *obtainment.* Christ was God's unspeakable gift to the world. The Holy Spirit was Christ's gift to His Church. I had been trying to do what the Holy Spirit *alone* could, and would, do for me. But I must receive Him by faith, on the ground of grace, and He would sanctify my heart, and apply the Blood, thus cleansing me from all sin and making the victory purchased by Christ on Calvary experiential. As I walked in the light as He was in the light, He would maintain the life of holiness and victory in my life day by day.

"It was all so wonderful and new to me. I had never heard such truth before. Oh, how my heart ached for just such a life, but I was hindered by fear of the consequences. I didn't want to be anything or do anything a Presbyterian ought not to be or do. I tried so hard to make the Lord see and understand my fears and feelings, but He had no sympathy for my fears. I couldn't make him a Presbyterian!

"The Salvation Army had come to our town. The Corps was composed of two wee girls in uniform. They held open-air meetings and made a noise with their tambourines. Their first soldier was a man called Daft Jimmy. He had hardly enough brains to give him a headache, but he had sense enough to get saved. He carried the flag as they marched the streets. On his jersey, a red one, he had the women put with white yarn these words on his back, 'Saved from public opinion.'

"I was told by Satan that I would have to go to the open-air meeting and march down the street with two wee girls and a fool. Maybe that didn't fill me with horrible dread! I would be laughed at by all my friends. I would loose my reputation.

"I said, 'Lord, I will be willing to go to Timbuctoo or Hong Kong, or even die decently as a martyr.' I couldn't get out of it. I became more and more miserable and, oh, so hungry for freedom and victory.

"At last I became desperate. The last night of the convention I saw it was a clean-cut, unconditional surrender; or continued wandering in failure, defeat and dissatisfaction. I left the meeting and went down to the shore, and there under a clear sky and shining stars I made the complete unconditional surrender. I cried out, 'Come in, come in Holy Spirit. Thy work of great blessing begin. By faith I lay hold of the promise, and claim complete victory over sin.'

"Hallelujah! What a thrill, what a peace, what a joy! Although an old-fashioned Presbyterian I began to weep and sing and rejoice like an old-fashioned Free Methodist. When I came home, I told my mother, "The surrender has been made, and I am free and so happy." She was delighted, for she told me she wondered whether I was really saved or not. She knew the blessing, for she had received it under the Rev. Andrew Murray's preaching held in a convention in Belfast. "The wonder to me was that all of the fear of what men might say or do had vanished, and now I was willing to do anything or go anywhere. The very thing I dreaded most before receiving the blessing, about the Salvation Army meeting, was faced. I couldn't say I was very happy about it; but I told the Lord I would do what He wanted, cost what it may. So I went to the open-air meeting on a Saturday night . . .

"As I walked down the street that Saturday it seemed as if every friend and relative I ever had were out and about. When I came to the open-air meeting and saw the two wee Salvation Army girls singing and rattling their tambourines, and poor Daft Jimmy holding the flag, I nearly turned back. Talk about dying! I was dying hard that night. I stepped off the footpath, and stood in the ring. The soldier looked at me. Then to my horror one of them said, 'The people don't stop and listen: let us get down on our knees and pray.' What could I do? I couldn't run away. So down I got on my knees.

"The crowd gathered around. I could hear their laughter and jeers. The officer prayed a telegram prayer - short and to the point. I could have wished the prayer had been as long as the 119th Psalm. I stood up, blushing and nervous. They got the collection while the crowd was there, and then to my horror, she said, 'Brother! take this tambourine and lead the march down the street to the Barracks.' I couldn't let a girl beat me, so I took it. That did it. My shackles fell of, and I was free; my fears all gone.

"I started down the street, whether in the body or out of the body, I can't tell. I lost my reputation, and fear of man: joy and peace and glory filled me. I can see now, and understand why the

Lord dealt with me so drastically. I would never, I believe, have come right through and out-and-out for Christ, in any other way. I was naturally timid and shy. I lost something that night I never want to find again, and I found something I never want to lose. That is, I lost my reputation and fear of man, and found the joy and peace of the overflowing fullness of the Spirit. Hallelujah!"

WAITING FOR GOD

Derick Bingham

DAILY HELP FOR THOSE WHO CAN'T SEE THE WOOD FOR THE TREES

400 pages £4.95

RUTH

Spencer Walton

UNDER THE SHADOW OF HIS WINGS

168 pages £2.95

THE TABERNACLE

Walter Scott

ITS STRUCTURE AND SYMBOLISM

176 pages £3.25

THE HEAVENLY FOOTMAN

John Bunyan

RUNNING THE RACE TO HEAVEN

64 pages £1.95

JOHN PLOUGHMANS TALK

C. H. Spurgeon

PLAIN ADVICE WITH PLENTY OF HUMOUR

128 pages £2.50

EFFECTIVE PRAYER
C. H. Spurgeon
AN INSPIRATIONAL CLASSIC
104 pages £2.25

THE WORD OF PROMISE
Horatius Bonar
A HANDBOOK TO THE PROMISES OF SCRIPTURE
305 pages £2.25

ROBERT MURRAY McCHEYNE
- A VIEW FROM THE PEW
William Lamb
EXTRACTS FROM AN ELDERS DIARY
160 pages £1.95

MORE THAN A DREAM
Derick Bingham
GOD'S HALL OF FAME - JOSEPH
96 pages £2.25